Liana

Her Story, My Words

An inspiring true story of courage and loss.

Di Goddard

ISBN 978-1-5272-3171-9

Printed and bound in the UK by Short Run Press Ltd

Cover design and layout © Di Goddard
Copyright thanks: Image of Liana © Di Goddard,
Purple butterfly © thwats @ Adobe Stock Images,
Blue flying butterflies © Vitalina Rybkova @ Adobe
Stock Images.

Donations from the sale of this book go to the
organ donation charity Liana was an advocate for
Live Life Give Life
www.livelifegivelife.org.uk

For Our Darling Li

7th June 1992 - 7th February 2015

11,923,542 minutes - each one of them a little crazy.

If love could have saved her,
she would have lived forever.

"When I told you I would travel the world to get to you, you see now that I meant it."

Mum x

Dedications

This book is dedicated to the memory of Liana Tolland, my beautiful eldest daughter, for whom twenty-two years was plenty enough.

To my youngest daughter Caitlin-Rose, who inspires me each day with her kind, gentle and witty personality. Who I look at with more love than she realises, although I will spend my life showing her. She is still able to live with an energy that blows my mind, she takes nothing for granted and if she wants a sofa day, she has one!

Also, for my husband Jay, who stands by my side in the funniest moments and the darkest hours. Unwavering with his love and strength, who also knows when I have cried enough; and tells me so!

Knowing that when we are three, we are still four.

Contents

Introduction

When you have a child, I guess you know there will be moments that are difficult. Sometimes parents will find themselves in a situation that they never anticipated, and there's always a deep instinct to protect your child.

When the situation calls for it and a parent must do the thing that they never thought possible, letting their child go, it is the betrayal of all things normal. There is no 'way' for it to happen that makes it okay; it will never be okay: so how does your heart find the strength to keep beating?

'It's not your story!' are four words that Liana said to me, early in her journey, that she maybe knew, maybe not, would be one of the reasons I am able to continue my own journey. It was when someone suggested I write about her story, as I had a history of working in publishing, that she leapt up and yelled, 'It's not your story!'

At that moment I realised that the feeling we get when we become parents is of an 'ownership' of our children: that they *belong* to us, and it is up to us to ensure their future, their safety, their life.

We forget that our life and our story belong to us, and not to our parents. So then, for our children, the story of their life belongs to them.

Of course we try to shape them and teach them right from wrong. But we cannot change their story and we can't stop them from leaving us when their time here is done, even if that is before us.

Their story is only a part of us, and doesn't belong to us. 'It's not your story!' – so then we must find the strength to let go of our guilt, our anger, and our frustration at their loss. We are powerless to play God even though we will want to.

We cannot get rid of our pain, but we can try and rise above some of the other pressures that we feel around our loss.

...

Of course, I have now decided it is the right time to share Liana's story in the hope even more people can be positively touched by her courage, her acceptance and her relentless journey to try and survive multi-organ failure at such a turning point in her life, as she went from being a teen to an adult.

I have considered well that there will be some who feel it is not right for me to share her story; and if this is you then this is perfectly fine, and you are free to pop the book back on the shelf. She wouldn't mind...

This book is for the benefit of those who have travelled a similar journey as a parent, or for those who are in the midst of the chaos and uncertainty that comes with having a life-limiting illness or a family member with one.

Or, you may wish to be encouraged to 'live your best life' (ugh I hate that phrase) by understanding more about the value of our time here on this Earth. Whatever reason you have chosen to read Liana's story, I hope you do so knowing that even when time is short, you can absolutely make it a great life. You can meet people that will change you forever. You can give something to others that you don't even know changed their day, how they felt about themselves, and what they knew.

People matter, nothing more... If I had to learn only one thing from losing my child then that is what I choose to take with me.

Oh, and if it makes you join the organ donor register too... Liana would say 'winner, winner, chicken, dinner'! She was a little odd like that...

Our Unit

I lost my daughter Liana. That's what I say, except to say I have 'lost' her implies I was careless, that I took my eye off her for a moment and she vanished...

It wasn't like that. I wouldn't have allowed that to happen, ever; this loss wasn't that reckless: this loss took place after four and a half years of desperately trying not to 'lose' her.

The fact is, Liana had lost; she had lost the will to go on, as I later found she had told our wonderful friend Caroline a few weeks before her death: she had had enough and was ready to leave. She seemed quite peaceful about it all even though I was a total wreck and unable to fathom a future without her in it. How ridiculous for her to be reassuring me!

We were a bit like that, she and I, reassuring each other. When one of us was in need, the other grew stronger and fought the battle and vice versa. My relationship with my second daughter Caitlin is now very similar. She too is a wonderful human being who amazes me with her strength and courage every day, and as soon as she sees me falter, she leaps up and saves the day! When she is in pain, I grow my strength wings and we battle on through the tsunami of grief that washes over us, so often without notice.

So, I didn't lose Liana, I guess. We fought like Trojans to the bitter end. She was a feisty number and I know that as I recount her story, it will bring laughter along with the inevitable tears.

Liana was born on 7th June 1992 to me, her 'single mother' of a parent. She arrived at 08.24 in the morning just as the sun came up, and was quickly whisked off down to special care as she was a tiny 4lbs 4oz and hadn't grown very strong. Two weeks of intensive care and we arrived home to start our bright but scary future together. This was the first time I fell in love.

As I was a nineteen-year-old Mum, Liana and I grew up together I suppose, learning how to be a family as we went. She was an energy-packed toddler and often wore the trousers in our mother-daughter relationship. She always knew what she wanted and was full of stomp and character. I later married and had Liana's little sister Caitlin four years later and our lives moved on as a family.

Liana was fiercely protective of her little sister, although that doesn't mean she didn't antagonise her daily. Poor Caitlin never had any peace and quiet, which she often craved as Liana was always on at her, bossing her around about something: but adore her she did.

Liana played the role of big sister well, especially in teaching Caitlin how to behave. This lesson was learned easily for Caitlin: simply watch your older sister do something wrong that earns her a telling off, and avoid behaving in this way yourself... Simple! Liana was a fine example of what not to do, but with it came much hilarity. If you were Caitlin's friend then you always knew Liana had an eye on you and you were not to hurt her. Imagine the scene for Caitlin's first boyfriend; he remembers vividly the moment he first met Liana, as she gave him the big sister talk and that was that. (It clearly worked as five years down the line they are still a great couple!).

Many years later as I went through my divorce with my first husband, Liana and Caitlin and I grew even closer: all girls together, and we became a strong little team. They were then aged twelve and eight. There is never the right time for this to happen in their lives, but they coped remarkably well. The girls always had their rules and boundaries from me, and Liana broke them, Caitlin didn't, having watched Liana's epic fails!

Liana was the kid that came home from the disco with a black eye, having fallen out with another girl... Her first-time drinking didn't go too well either... She was all systems go, all the time! It was that adventurous spirit that is probably the reason one of her teachers at school gave her some leaflets about gap-years when she was seventeen. It was information about an educational charity on a remote island off the west coast of Scotland and she came home brandishing leaflets. I knew from the first minute she would go, that was just so Liana. Just grab life by the hands and squeal with excitement along the way!

She had to raise a few thousand pounds to fund her project and started that by organising a sky-dive with friends (who were also my friends, but I wasn't daft enough to jump out of a plane with them!) – I can still hear her screaming, "Woo-hoooo" as she leapt from the plane, before I could even see her through the clouds! The excitement was clear for everyone on the ground to hear. Of course, Liana would jump out of a plane... Why not?!

She went on a couple of training weeks on the remote Isle of Coll, flying up to Glasgow and taking the train across the country to the ferry: even crossing on the ferry was traumatic so set her up for some exciting memories over those weeks. She met lots of wonderful new friends and became more and more excited about her adventure abroad as it came closer.

Uganda

Liana had started a blog early on to both fundraise for the trip and to tell her story during the year away. Here is the text from that blog, her words and then her first and only blog from Uganda:

Hello! My name is Liana Tolland & I am going to Uganda for one year with the charity Project Trust. I'm leaving 3rd September 2010 from Heathrow & I get to stop off in Dubai on the way. There's going to be a lot of travelling to actually get to my destination but there are 21 volunteers in total off to Uganda! I have two partners that I'll be living with for the duration of the year, Rosie & Leyna.

My project is called Queen of Peace & I will be teaching at the Queen of Peace School situated in a small rural village in Muge. Things are pretty basic & the school only has 3-4 full time staff! I will also be living in the same village as the school. Electricity is pretty much non-existent & water is from a pond-like thing apparently. Shocked.

I'm soo excited to start my journey & I hope to go traveling within Uganda on my holidays. I don't really know much about my project so I guess I'll just find out when I get there!

Hopefully I will be able to get internet access when I travel into Kampala and keep eveyone updated on here...so fingers crossed.

Love Liana xXx

She was to go to Uganda, to a project called Queen of Peace, about two hours away from the capital Kampala. Very remote, and accessible by boda boda (motorcycle taxi). The flight out was on 3rd September 2010 and we set off with my stomach in knots and hers full of excitement. She was raring to go and full of all the vaccinations she would require for such an environment. A week before she left she started taking the anti-malarial tablets Doxycycline, recommended as there was a history of depression in our family so Malarone wasn't advised.

We arrived to meet the other 20 Ugandan volunteers at Terminal 3, London Heathrow at midday. Liana already knew that once they arrived in Uganda they would all spend the first night with hosts James and Isobel in the capital and then the next day they would all split off to their projects. Liana had been placed with two other young girls, Leyna and Rosie whom she met for the first time at the airport.

She looked so tiny, standing in her jeans, a blue and white stripy tee-shirt, and Converse trainers, hair tied back in braids, knowing that she wasn't likely to get to wash it in a long time! She could take as much as she could fit into a huge rucksack, the type the army carry. It was quite possibly taller than she was! She couldn't even lift it and shrieks of laughter came at each attempt. Lots of help was needed from the taller boys, I know.

There was so much excitement and anticipation as they all started to identify that they were part of the Uganda team. Anxiety too, but mainly from the parents of all these young bewildered eighteen-year olds about to fly off for a whole year! Contact was to be intermittent at best. Liana tried to reassure me that if I didn't hear from her that it was okay, she would be able to write me a letter and perhaps a few weeks into the trip could get to Kampala and find a way of calling home!! What?? I was petrified, what if something happened? What if she needed me? What if she died out there? You hear that can happen, don't you?!

It was possible that I was able to visit the project in the Spring of the next year, but I was only to come if I brought a suitcase of Mars Bars and clean pants!

I wasn't sure how to tackle a whole year without Liana, so saying a final goodbye was ridiculously hard. She dealt with it by being totally cool and showing me that I was being a bit daft, as it was, 'Only a year Mum.' So, we hugged and kissed goodbye, and I walked away, but as I looked back at her I had this overwhelming desire to go back and hug her again, like I wouldn't see her again, so I did, and as I bawled my eyes out she just said 'It's okay Mum, I will be okay'...

I was walked out of the airport by a friend and Liana's boyfriend, and sobbed pretty much the whole way home to Yeovil. I tracked the flight through Dubai and a quick change on to Entebbe, Uganda. Radio silence... I could see the plane had landed but that was it. The year started, and I was without her.

I got on with working and being a Mum to Caitlin and partner to Jay. It was eerily silent without her around. Really quiet! No mess! Less washing! We could only guess at the time she was having, so far away from home.

The first contact came in the form of a text message a couple of days later simply saying, 'Found signal, am alive, nearly died on the back of a boda (motorbike) and I love it here'.

Oh my God, a link to her – I replied quickly with a text and said, 'Stay safe, I love you Li, I miss you'... then she went back to the school.

About three weeks later I had a random message from her via Facebook. She had gone into the city and was at an internet café.

'Mum, it's me, I am okay, I ate fish head soup, everyone is lovely, the children are amazing, Leyna and Rosie are fab, I haven't washed for weeks and the toilet is a hole in the ground next to a pig sty'

... there was so much news for her to tell me, but mostly her excitement was that we had set up a webcam in my office facing the kitchen and given her a web link to log onto so she could see home, and she wrote in capital letters 'I CAN SEE YOU!!!!'. Oh my, I was a crying wreck and held up a sign that said, 'I Love You!' scribbled on A4 paper I whipped out of my printer with speed.

We spoke via web chat for a few minutes until her internet token ran out: she was able to Facebook me a few photos she had taken on her digital camera and I learned more and more as each minute went by.

They lived on rice (mainly fried!) and full-fat coke (good God, child!) and her role out there was to

teach English and Drama (she was full of drama so
that suited her well) and the girls lived in a concrete
shack with a tin roof and a blue door. There was a
little separation between the living and sleeping
areas but ultimately it was a dusty dirty mess - they
had managed to put up some mosquito nets over
their beds, but one had a hole in it already! My
nerves were getting worse by the minute!

There were pictures of family and friends all over
the walls and the girls created a bond. They sang
songs and had so many funny stories to tell. Water
collecting was perilous and water purifying tablets
were to be used always, hence the vast amounts of
coke being consumed. Liana had warned me she
would come home as fat as a pig by the end of the
year as everything was fried in oil - everything!

It was incredible to have her messages. I felt a
spark in her, she was alive, and it gave me such joy.

Blog number one soon followed ...

Kampala, Uganda
Oct 8, 2010

*Hi guys!! I have about 10 mins left in which to fill you in
on the past month, so hopefully it works...here goes...*

*I've had some real mad times eating fish heads,
plucking chickens and what not (usual really haha).
iv been seriously ill n they thought it was malaria.
Turns out to be a urine infection :S I've invested in an
African dress called a Gomesi. Have seen Leyna run
for her life across the floor naked because someone
walked into the house when she was washing. I've*

been spotted with no clothes on due to forgetting that Africans like to walk right in. And I've been asked to be married on many occasions haha...

Rosie and Leyna, my partners, are pretty legendary. We sing our way through the days and have some riot laughing. Last night Henry my next door neighbour had to use a needle to extract a jigga from my toe (small very painfull bug thing) and I have made some amazing friends 4 life :) Sorry its quick and short but my time has come to an end. Will update u soon. love u and miss u england xxxxx

Radio silence again until another three weeks later. I could not believe it: on a Wednesday afternoon, my mobile phone showed 'Liana Uganda Phone' on the screen! I was working from home and the phone was on my desk next to me. I leapt up and screamed 'Liana??'

I heard her voice and started crying again, with joy. She had randomly checked her phone and picked up a roaming mobile phone signal and called me immediately.

She was telling me about having been sick for the last 24 hours, that she must have picked up a bug and had been throwing up all night, but it was okay as Leyna and Rosie were looking after her and she would be fine. 'Just make sure Mum that if you come out, you bring chocolate and noodles and clean everything, as we are filthy!'...

A few moments later one of her room-mates came onto the phone and said Liana was off being sick again so she would talk to me until she came back...

It made me anxious, but I expected I would feel this way many times over the year and I talked myself down. I asked, 'Is she okay do you think?' and was reassured that they had all had it at some stage, so it was just Liana's turn!

A few minutes later Liana came back on the phone and we said our goodbyes. I made her promise me she would sip water and not get dehydrated and asked her please to call me back when she could.

I was so elated to have spoken to her and did all the rounds calling family and her boyfriend to tell them she was okay - well, vomiting, but okay!

I felt quite anxious about her being sick, but had heaps of reassurance from family and friends that she would be fine, so eventually I took this in and just enjoyed the fact I had spoken with her on the phone.

The Call Nobody Wants To Get

Thursday 14th October 2010.

A normal working day... until 4pm and the home phone rang. It took a moment to digest what was being said and I don't think I worried at first. It was the Director of the charity that had organised Liana's placement in Uganda telling me that Liana had been taken to a medical centre overnight as she had been extremely sick. They were worried about her and I was told to expect a call from the medical insurance doctors next. I felt the panic start to rise inside my stomach. But I told myself that she would be okay and be back at camp in a day or two.

I then spoke with a doctor from the insurance company in London who had been in direct contact with the clinic doctor in Kampala, an English representative who was the point of contact for the charity. He was the first person to knock my legs out from under me as he told me that Liana was in grave danger and extremely unwell, but they could not ascertain why.

They would be in close contact over the next twenty-four hours but they said that we must prepare for the worst. Of course, I asked the awful question, 'Is she going to die?', to which he replied, 'At this time I am unable to say'...

Panic fed its way through my core, I remember starting to feel heat rise through me, like a hot sweat. I couldn't take this in. I thought he would say 'NO, NO, OF COURSE SHE WON'T DIE...' Why didn't he say that? What did he mean, he was unable to say if she would die or not?

I sat on the step in the kitchen... He had promised he would call with any more information and gave me all the relevant contact details. Liana was in good hands and they were doing all they could. 'Doing all they could' sounded like something out of a TV hospital drama: why did he say that?

I felt the room spinning and immediately called my husband Jay, who was taking his mother to a hospital appointment in London, at least three hours away from our home. I think I was so hysterical he didn't know what I was saying or what I was even asking him to do. It was all a little crazy and he said he would call me after dropping his mother off and when he was heading home on the motorway.

It all felt very dramatic, slightly unreal, and I stumbled across the road to a friend Jane and banged on her door bawling my eyes out, and she let me sit for a while and tried as best she could to calm me down and be hopeful for a good outcome. The next few hours seemed totally unreal, phone calls to family and friends, to Liana's boyfriend who was at University. Everyone was starting to see the panic in me and I could feel their anxiety too.

Family started to arrive at the house and I received another call at 8pm to say that Liana was going down for surgery to operate, as they needed to identify the problem and that it might be peritonitis. I would receive a phone call in one hour to update me.

My parents were at the house, Jay arrived home, Caitlin was back from school and we all sat anxiously waiting for any update. Inevitably when an hour later the phone didn't ring I started to go into meltdown and think the worst. I was inconsolable and kept asking if people thought she was going to die out there! I wanted reassurance, like a child, hoping for someone to say, 'There, there, it will all be okay', except nobody did that, nobody.

At about 10pm the phone finally rang, and the doctor fed back the information that Liana had not had surgery, as a last-minute blood test had come through to say that she had pancreatitis and that if they had operated they would have killed her.

She had got as far as having a general anaesthetic and being in the operating theatre when this news came through. Pancreatitis, okay pancreatitis... But, she was extremely ill. She had stopped urinating and they were feeding a tube into her bladder but were unable to release any urine, and what they had thought on an x-ray was a full bladder that needed emptying was in fact a sac of fluid in her abdomen caused by the pancreatitis, and that really her bladder was empty, which implied that her kidneys had shut down too.

*** From Liana's point of view:

Liana remembered this time very well. Later she told me that she remembered being taken to the clinic by worried friends and rolling in and out of consciousness, agonising stomach pain waking her and then passing out again. She had never known pain like it. Vomiting and screaming in equal measure.

She remembered being wheeled into theatre and told she was going to have an operation, and that she felt extreme fear as she couldn't understand a word anyone was saying except the British doctor: everyone else was Ugandan and the place seemed short of equipment and comfort.

Then she remembered being told she was being medically evacuated out of Uganda into Kenya and that she had to wait for a team to become available to transport her there. She was moved onto the plane twelve hours later, and the only part she remembers is being on a stretcher and looking up to see the pilot's face smiling down at her and telling her they were off, and it might be a bumpy ride... Then she lapsed back into unconsciousness.

***

Back home in the UK, well, we didn't sleep of course. I was up all night pacing, waiting for news of when she was being flown out of the country. There was a hold up, as the medical evacuation team were just returning from another flight and were made to rest before they could fly again, so for what seemed like eons of time, we waited, and we waited.

We were told not to make any arrangements to go to Kenya until we knew she had arrived there alive. Why did they keep implying she might not survive? It was a torture of truths that I was unable to comprehend. The medical insurance company would arrange flights, but the insurance covered only one parent, so we would have to find the money for Jay to accompany me.

Eventually, Liana was flown overnight on Friday and we eventually heard of her safe arrive in Nairobi at 8am on the Saturday morning, by which time her boyfriend had arrived from university and I had made arrangements for Caitlin (who was then 14) to stay with her Dad.

Jay and I drove to Heathrow to catch a Saturday evening flight. It was a slow burning torture. The scary part about being on the flight was that there would be zero communication for the duration, approximately eight hours. We were placed in First Class seating, which was simply because we asked to be seated together if it was at all possible as I was totally out of control of my emotions and the booked seats were a few rows apart. We waited until everyone had boarded. The stewards even asked a couple of people if they would mind moving their seat, so we could be seated together but people didn't want to move: God forbid they might lose out? I didn't understand it, but I lost a little faith in humanity right there. Anyway, someone was looking after us as suddenly, the steward said she had two free seats in First Class, so we were moved there.

It seemed so ridiculously ironic. We could never have afforded to fly First Class at that time, so to have such luxury but be totally unable to find any enjoyment in it was almost laughable. Jay pulled his bed out and slept, once he had had some nourishment, the lights were turned out for the night flight and I just sat staring out of my window. It must have been about 4am when I saw big swathes of lightening fire across the black sky. It felt incredibly peaceful, but I was shaking.

The Virgin stewards were incredibly kind, and I got chatting to one who came and sat at the foot of my pull-out bed. He was funny and caring, and brought me food and asked me please to try and eat something, but I felt sick. I cried some more and eventually the daytime came, and we landed at Nairobi airport.

Arriving in Kenya

We stumbled our way through the airport: it felt surreal. We carried just a bag of clean clothes and our washbags. We were told to wait for a taxi that was sent to take us to the hotel opposite Nairobi hospital. As we got to the security control we were given passes to enter the country under a medical emergency.

This whole environment was alien. Having never travelled to Africa previously we were totally out of our depth. The roads were so dusty, and it penetrated your throat along with the energy-sapping heat. We came with jeans and tops and stood out like a sore thumb. Not to mention that Jay is a 6ft tall Englishman with a shaved head!

It appeared that we were expected, and of course we were treated like royalty. It felt as though everyone was trying to impress upon us how they were here to help us, which was reassuring. The taxi driver informed us he was to take us not directly to the hospital as we had thought but to a hotel. But I wanted to go straight to Liana: this was not allowed, so we arrived at the hotel and were told to check in and then we could walk to the hospital as it was directly over the road. He reassured us it would be one minute away.

Bags dumped, we practically ran out of the hotel doors and across the road. Jay managed to squeeze in a cigarette as we headed across the road, and it was chaotic. Massive holes in the road and pavements, road signs at head height, and there was no health and safety apparent here!

A woman sat with a new-born baby at the hotel entrance on the side of the road, begging for money, and the security guards all held huge guns aloft. It was the other side of the world in more ways than one! We found the hospital across the road and went in by the back gates and through the car park, with rows and rows of dust-covered cars, endless bicycles and everything padlocked to within an inch of its life!

The concrete buildings were dishevelled and chaotic, and a hand-painted sign on a wall pointed up a set of concrete stairs to a wooden door at the top. It said ICU: we knew this was our destination. I seemed to be a few steps ahead of Jay the whole time, just racing ahead to get to her. I felt my heart in my chest banging hard against my rib-cage, and I thought I could pass out at any moment. The excitement of seeing her for the first time in six weeks was dulled by the fear of what we were about to walk into.

As we got to the top of the steps and opened the door, the room was full of Kenyans, all chatting, some praying. It was rammed with people and was clearly a waiting room. As a nurse walked though I grabbed her arm and said, 'Do you know where my daughter is please?" and she said, 'Who is your daughter?" I thought the fact we were the only white people in the room may have given that away, but it seemed not! 'Liana Tolland' I said without hesitation, and she said, 'I will take you'.

We pushed our way through the crowded waiting room and through a set of double doors. Immediately to our right was another set of doors, the entrance to ICU: and before we took another step forward, I saw Liana's bright green Jack Wills bag under the bottom of a hospital bed. The head of the bed was not visible and was right behind the door. I later was told, they didn't have space in ICU for her, so they made a space by closing one of the double doors and placing her bed behind it!

I thought I couldn't feel my legs under me but somehow, I got through the room and next to her. I can see her little face now, bright red with the heat, doped up with pain drugs and hooked up to odd-looking machines. We both started to cry, and held each other. The nurse sitting at the end of her bed quietly got up and left.

Liana told me that that nurse had told her that her parents were coming on a flight. She was so scared that when the nurse finished her shift in the evening, she had sat with her all night until we got there! I was overwhelmed with gratitude for her compassion, but she had already gone, with no thanks expected.

Within a short period of time we had met Dr Silverstein, an American doctor who oversaw Liana's care and much else in the hospital. He was brutally honest with us, asking us to follow him into a cramped and cluttered side room office filled with filing cabinets. I sat on the only chair, and Jay stood behind me. It was at this point I realised that nobody was going to tell me it was going to be okay, nobody... Dr Silverstein was giving us the truth.

Liana was in a very serious condition. She had suffered with haemorrhagic pancreatitis and was not doing well; her kidneys had shut down and her body was in shock. He wasn't sure that she was going to survive and the next few days were critical.

There it was. Nothing nice.

I walked out into the garden below the steps to the ICU unit and knelt on the grass and howled with pain. I had so many thoughts racing through my mind that I couldn't even decide which one to focus on. I felt sick. My whole future was being endangered by the fact that I could lose her! This was not meant to happen to me, to us, to her... This was not part of the deal.

I called my mother, who was away at the time, on her mobile phone and I think the one sentence I could get out was along the lines of, 'She's going to fucking die, Mum'. That was it... I was hysterical and had no understanding of how this could be happening and why I couldn't stop it, get off the ride, step off the world, if it would only stop long enough for me to do that.

Bracing ourselves for the coming days was terrifying: not just because we were so far away from home and the loving support of family and friends but because this was just too much to take on board. My mind couldn't process any of it.

Liana was hooked up to monitors and drips and medication, endless drugs and a constant gentle dialysis called filtering, I learned. Little did I know that in the coming years I would become something of a medical whiz, able to use all the terms and names that

I previously didn't know existed (and didn't want to know).

We sat with Liana all day and into the evening, helping her when she was in pain and talking to her and reminding her that everything was going to be okay. She was most upset in the knowledge that regardless of what happened next, Uganda was over, she was not going back, it just wasn't happening. She cried so hard; she had wanted to do this year for so long, so we told her that she could go back another year and we left the conversation there.

She was so scared by what had happened that it quickly became clear that she needed to get back home.

Back at the hotel room, we tried to sleep, but it really didn't happen. We spent ages on the phone in the hotel room to Liana's Grandad in the USA who wanted regular updates and detailed accounts of course. He was reassuring us all the time and we were so grateful for his love. Family were all trying to understand what was happening and to try and take in the seriousness of this whole situation.

I had a yearning to be at home looking after Caitlin. Contact with her was limited. There was no way I wanted her to think for a second that her big sister might die, so we didn't tell the truth about the situation in Kenya. Lying was very easy when it came to protecting her.

We headed back to the ICU at the crack of dawn the next day. Liana had been moved to the other side of the ICU unit as a bed space had become free, sadly. The gentleman who had been smiling at her the day before had passed away. We were aware that something had happened that morning as we approached through the yard. A large group of Kenyans were singing, praying, wailing and ultimately honouring the life of a loved one. It was an incredible sight to witness, slightly overwhelming but a real show of love and affection and, I think, acceptance of the passing, thanking God, asking for peace.

When we entered the ICU, there she was, but she was surrounded by some of the members of the deceased's family: they all held hands around her bed and were praying aloud together for her. I didn't understand what they were doing and cautiously walked over. They explained that they wanted their prayers to be passed to Liana so that God would heal her, as their loved one no longer needed their support. Jay and I joined hands with them and it made me cry as they prayed. Liana was crying too, filled up with their love.

I couldn't imagine this happening at a hospital in the UK, so it was lovely to feel so wrapped in their love and prayers and I had hoped it would provide a miracle for us, that maybe God would listen to their prayers if mine weren't good enough!

They dispersed later in the day, but still now all these years later this time holds a profound memory for me. It was the start of my understanding that whatever happens, people matter, nothing else, just people. Only fellow humans can help you, love you, fix you, stand by you... whether rich or poor, white or black, everyone matters, people matter.

We took occasional breaks from our bedside vigil, but rarely. We were told by the doctors to go and have a break and were often sent back to the hotel for a sleep, but we really couldn't sleep at all. Jay would fall asleep and I would leap back up and cross the road again.

After lunch that day, we had gone back to the hotel to freshen up, and when we came back, all hell was let loose. From behind the curtains closed around Liana's bed, we could hear her screaming out in pain, surrounded by doctors. I felt my legs go from under me and somehow, we got the attention of a doctor who said they were trying to control Liana's pain as it had started again in her pancreas.

It took about an hour of pandemonium before they managed to knock her out and calm her down: she had been given some very powerful drugs and we were asked once again to come in to the doctor's office. He confessed that he was not sure whether she was responding to their treatment. I clearly looked as though I was unable to cope and on the verge of collapse, because the doctor asked us to come to his main office that afternoon, which we did.

He said he would support us all he could, and his main aim was to get Liana back onto UK soil. He gave me some strong sleeping tablets and told me to go and rest before I ended up as an inpatient too! He also took an opportunity to speak with Jay about his smoking! He had seen us walk across the car park that morning, Jay puffing away, and he didn't like this one bit, and was very stern.

I realised I was no longer able to function, so took the tablets and slept for a few hours. When we came back, Liana was much more rested too and was responding well to the different drugs. She still had zero kidney function and our focus was that the kidneys needed to be working for us to get back to the UK. They had managed to drain the huge fluid build-up in her abdomen and she was more comfortable now. It was still touch and go, we knew that, but we felt stronger and needed to battle on together.

Every day brought more knowledge about what was happening to Liana. Tests were done for the obvious causes like malaria, and other tropical diseases, but everything came back clear. The kidneys were mysteriously not functioning, and we prayed and did every rain dance under the sun. Liana's health problems became a focus for all our friends and family back home too, and they all sent messages of love and support.

The hotel became our second home: it provided no frills, but we didn't want to spend any time there except to sleep. Eating was basic, but we had no appetite. We washed our clothes and underwear in the bathroom sink, and I took Liana's bag of bits back and tried to wash through it too, using shower gel and soap. The clothes she had been transported in were thick with brown dust from the Ugandan countryside. The water in the tap was boiling hot and you could hardly touch it (no health and safety here, remember) and it took basin after basin to get the clothing anywhere near clean... She had a pair of rubber flip flops that she told me had been made from old car tyres, handmade in Uganda. One size fits all but probably not her tiny size 3 feet.

Prayers

Suddenly, we had been in Nairobi for a week. The day-to-day struggle to understand and integrate into the alien environment had passed. We were no longer petrified of the machine gun toting security guards at the hotel entrance; they asked why we were here and every day wanted to know how our baby was doing: was there news? I hoped one day they would meet her, that we would be able to bring her back to the hotel with us. Of course, that never happened but their friendship and prayers were added to the list of help we received.

We befriended the hotel staff; we became regulars, sadly. Liana's health became of interest to everyone there, and gifts were sent over to the hospital. One beautiful receptionist, a tiny lady called Terri, asked to come over to the ICU one day and we obliged. She cried when she saw Liana and said to her, 'You have to get well, little girl, and go home to the UK, we all love you'... Liana had been told!

I managed to locate a small room in the hotel used as a prayer room. I spent a while there each day. It was more like a broom cupboard, with a solitary window high up and a small cross on the opposite wall. Chairs were fitted in tightly together, two rows of four. It was the beginning of feeling drawn to any room with a cross and hint of religion. I threw out many prayers, begging almost, praying, 'Just don't take her from me' and hoping that was enough to save her life.

I met the hospital priest, Father James, who was Irish and with a thick accent. He had been trying to locate me for a few days, having heard of Liana, and we met in a corridor: I was of course identifiable by the colour of my skin. We sat together for a while in the waiting area of the ICU and I cried beside him.

He spoke very openly and honestly about the risk of death, and I found again that he wasn't going to be the one to pat me on the head and tell me that everything would be all right. We prayed together but I mainly cried. I could see how my fear was affecting Jay, and how much pain it gave him on top of his own anxiety. Father James was in demand elsewhere, and he went off to do his duties. He left us with his contact details and promised to come back daily, which he did.

We never left Liana's side except to sleep, but that was very little and sporadic. It was like a torture, just wanting her to get well again.

Ten days into her treatment, it was deemed that Liana was well enough to try and leave the ICU and go to a private room in the hospital. It was a wonderful relief to feel that she was strong enough to be moved to a room. Her bed was wheeled out of the ICU and down a stream of long corridors. We felt as though we were in a fish bowl with everyone looking in, as people couldn't help but stare at this sick British girl and her pale, exhausted family.

I remember her being wheeled past an indoor therapy room with a small therapy pool and saying to me how she would kill to be in that water. Her bed was pushed up the ramps to the top floor of the private wing. There was nothing like the NHS here and thankfully our medical insurance covered her care for as long as it took, but of course our main aim was to make it back to the UK.

As we rose to the top of the slopes on which the hospital was built it became increasingly exhausting, and we were reminded that the air was very thin this far above sea level (at nearly 1,800 metres). We were sweating and panting, except Liana who was like Lady Muck being wheeled around.

One of her nurses, Stephen, came with us and spent some time helping her settle in. He had a huge impact on both Liana and me as his care was incredible. He was intrigued to hear her stories of life back in England and we chatted for a long time. He was loving and very kind, and I do wonder if she had him over a barrel at one stage, when I found him peeling grapes for her to eat! Very Liana!

I was provided with a bed in the private room with Liana, as we had earlier made the decision that Jay would head back to the UK to arrange the repatriation, now that she was out of imminent danger. We had spoken to the medical insurance company who preferred Liana to stay in Kenya to receive her care. We foresaw that it would be a struggle to get her back on UK soil, so reluctantly we arranged a flight for Jay and agonisingly for us all he left, were distraught at his departure.

He didn't want to leave us both there, but we were aware of all that needed looking after at home especially Caitlin and also the dog, left in the care of neighbours who had kindly jumped in as we rushed away. Also, as we were both self-employed, one of us had to start earning some money again, and we really didn't know how long this situation would last. I felt anxious about being on my own with Liana, but this was not the time nor place for wimps. The hospital provided me with meals and the bed for me in Liana's room was comfortable. But I slept very little and tended to Liana as well as I could.

She had no need to go to the bathroom as she still had no kidney function and had been unable to eat (other than peeled grapes) for the two weeks since she had been ill. During that first two weeks she dropped down from a size 14 to a size 8/10 fast. Her body started to become unrecognisable and as I bathed her one night she said she could feel her bones through her bottom in the bath! So, we shuffled her out, every move was slow, and she had zero energy.

Her nephrologist (kidney doctor) in Kenya was a funny and cheerful man called Dr Ernest Kyoko. He had a wonderful aftershave smell and Liana used to tell him 'you smell lovely'... He was a grandfatherly figure and used to smile and laugh all the time. His was a positive energy and he used to say to us continually that her kidneys would wake up when they wanted to. We really believed this, and it gave us hope, which was pretty much all we were left with.

Doctors came regularly, and Liana slept most of the time. She was a little sick every now and then when she tried to eat, but otherwise it was a case of, 'Come on kidneys, wake up'! We had everyone back home doing rain dances: anything to get us out of there.

It became apparent that the kidneys should have started working by that stage, and that we needed to consider how to get her back to the UK for treatment.

Her health was so poor at this time that she was not deemed fit enough for a medical evacuation which would have involved stops in different countries on a smaller private plane. It was a difficult one to work out.

Jay was on home soil pushing for her to be brought home, and had a real fight on his hands as nobody wanted her moved. But, she wanted to come home to the UK hospitals, and so fight we did. Eventually it was cleared for a senior consultant from the UK to fly over to Kenya and to bring us back escorted on a Virgin Airways flight, which would mean eight hours of travelling, during which Liana would be supervised and medicated by the consultant.

We waited another two days for him to arrive and rest overnight. We knew which flight we were booked on and we got Liana into a wheelchair and down to a waiting car, taking us to the airport twenty miles away. She wasn't strong enough to walk but we could get a wheelchair at the airport to move her onto the plane.

This is where the chaos started: as we headed out onto the highway, we discovered an annual marathon was being held and all the major roads were closed.

We became stuck, in miles of traffic, dust and heat – and it soon became obvious we weren't getting to the airport any time soon. The consultant used every which way he could to get us on that flight. It was the most hideous car journey. We were driving on pavements, across fields, Liana and I were being hurled around like rag dolls in the back of the car and the driver was protesting, saying we must go back. The consultant said very clearly that we had to make it to the flight or Liana would not make the journey back to the UK, and that this was our one chance... no pressure then!

Liana didn't take this news well and we started to get upset. A call was made to the airport and as we watched the clock go way past the time of take-off, we had been assured that the plane would not take off without us. Something, I am sure, to do with the screaming that went on in the front of the car as the consultant said, in no uncertain terms, if you take off without her you will likely kill her.

We drove around the periphery of the airport and could see the Virgin plane still on the tarmac waiting. Oh my God! So, the driver pulled up and ran off to get a wheelchair with the consultant in tow, Liana and I were left on our own in the car, so I said to her, 'You have a choice, you can miss the plane, or we can try and run', so that's what we did. I hauled her out of the car and put my arm under her and around her back and we ran, crying with laughter as she hadn't walked for two weeks and had zero strength, her legs buckling and twisting. Quickly the consultant came with the wheelchair and she fell into it and we headed for Departures.

The drama wasn't over. The consultant was delayed at check-in and security, as he carried a defibrillator which had to be painstakingly taken out of its case and reviewed, piece by piece.

At this point I could be seen wheeling Liana onto the plane minus the consultant, because at this stage I really thought the plane would take off without us!

First class it was, then: we took up most of everyone's space with medical equipment, and restrictions were in place so that people couldn't walk up the aisle on our side as the consultant had made a makeshift drip stand by lodging a pencil into the overhead locker. Very technical! We got into the air and felt slightly euphoric at the thought that we would make it back to the UK, we were bound for home.

Home Soil & Brutal Truths

A bed had been found for Liana at our closest renal unit, at Dorset County Hospital in the pretty market town of Dorchester. As we hit the tarmac at London Heathrow, Liana and I held hands: she was in the seat behind me, with the consultant across the aisle. I put my hand over the headrest behind me and she grabbed it and started to cry.

We waited to be the last ones off the plane, and an ambulance was waiting for us at the terminal, so that we could be taken to Dorchester. Handover complete, we were on our way, and she slept like a baby the whole way there whilst I rang everyone and got things in place.

Jay met us at the hospital and we were taken to the renal ward. As Liana was taken to a private room I started to shake and felt as though the room was spinning, so a lovely nurse came with a chocolate biscuit and a cup of tea. I think I relaxed for the first time in two full weeks and my body was just as worn out as my mind, unable to cope with much more of this.

That hospital was somewhere Liana would spend lots of time in the coming months, and it appeared that our problems were far from over. I had rested at home that first night and come back the next morning to find her sitting in bed putting French plaits in her hair, looking quite smiley and happy. Still no kidney function and she was set up to have dialysis three times a week. She was being looked after by a lovely team and we were slowly introduced to the routine that would become normal over the following weeks.

By day three everything seemed to change. I arrived to find Liana in floods of angry tears, totally anxious and not coping, which was truly a shock at this point! Liana had been in a consultation with her nephrologist who had asked her about her future plans.

Liana told her she had always wanted to join the police force, and quite abruptly the consultant told her, 'You can kiss that goodbye' and it seemed to spiral Liana mentally out of control. The stark reality of what had happened but also what was in her future, had been served up like a dish of cold dinner for her to digest with zero emotional support and not even with a parent or friend to comfort her.

She had been told that there was now very little chance her kidneys would ever work again and that she would need medical attention and a transplant, and to forget any major plans that she had made... She would possibly need a pancreas transplant also.
Boom, another massive jolt for the emotions.

I know for a fact that this was the day that Liana's mental health took a turn for the worse. She had gone from being told by the nephrologist in Nairobi that she would be fine and of course her kidneys would start again, 'Don't worry your pretty face' (and of course we held onto that like anything), to being told the bleak truth, and it hurt: she didn't like it, I didn't like it, it was too much to swallow after the last couple of weeks, and it felt as though we were losing control.

Didn't this happen to other people?

Liana was inconsolable and understandably she was angry and upset by the whole world and the fact that this could even happen to her. It was simply too much for her to process.

She became snappy and tearful and was being sick also, which we thought was a side effect of having no kidney function and needing dialysis. She had started to eat a little although was still losing weight at a rapid rate. She kept no food down and it was just an exhausting time.

We spent lots of time over the coming days firing questions at anyone who would listen; she incessantly rang the buzzer to ask for help. Both she and the situation had spiralled out of control.

On reflection, I understand her response. But at the time it was as though the ferocious and determined young girl I had seen off at the airport two months earlier, who had survived so much shit so far, had finally started to turn into an anxious wreck with every sign of being mentally destroyed.

Googling is a modern-day nightmare: it should be banned for anything medical. If I listened to Google, then I could find any answer I wanted. All manner of experiences and outcomes were described online. Of course I was cheered by some of the happy endings, but there were others that became the stuff of nightmares.

I hardly slept thinking up all the horrors and found myself begging God again not to take her away from me. As soon as I woke, I jumped in my car and drove the 20 miles to spend the day with her, to help her, to soothe her, wash her, make her get dressed, anything!

She had some kind nurses who really took a beating from her banging on that bloody buzzer every five minutes. I can now look back and see she was having the first in a series of emotional breakdowns, but at the time it was all so complicated and painful to watch.

I felt that she had been placed in the wrong ward. Her situation seemed more acute than others with renal problems, and I wasn't convinced that the staff had enough expertise (or time) to take on her case. Liana wasn't just a renal patient, she had a multitude of problems, but because she needed dialysis she had been placed here. I am so sad to have felt like that as the staff did all that they could. But her case was quite exceptional, and she needed complex care by a team with experience of pancreatic care as well.

These of course, are simply my personal thoughts now and not a reflection of her care at that time.

She was still vomiting and not keeping much down, and this was stopping her from coming home. She was now being taken down to the dialysis unit in the hospital for her sessions three times a week. I know how hard she found this as all the patients down there were older, much older; there was one lady in her thirties but otherwise it felt like a totally alien experience for her.

I guess this was starting to become a time when she realised that this was how her life was going to be – it was total torture for her and there was no getting away from it.

It was a tough age to become this sick. At eighteen you are considered an adult, but only on a technicality.

I feel that her care should have been a little more sympathetic to her age as an adult/child and that she shouldn't have been expected to take things on board as an adult would, or perhaps it would have been this bad for her at thirty? I am not sure!

She befriended a few of the nurses and other patients and I think they genuinely cared for her and could see her fear. A couple of the old girls would sit and chat with her while she dialysed. Dialysis never made her feel better, just totally exhausted her and made her feel sick; everyone copes differently though. Her body was tiny by now and it was a hard physical and emotional situation to live with.

After a month in the hospital, I became a normal part of the furniture too. Where she was, I was. I couldn't stand to leave her side and she didn't want me to be apart from her either, I suppose. She had lots of other visitors, both family and close friends, but it really took its toll on all of us.

I arrived one morning, and Liana was already at dialysis. I knew this as she had phoned me from the dialysis unit to ask me if I was arriving soon. She sounded anxious and I assured her I was only thirty minutes away.

I arrived with the normal bag of goodies, snacks, things to do and headed straight for the unit. Liana was clearly anxious and had a nurse sitting with her. She was breathing into a paper bag and hunched forward into her raised knees. I reassured her and tried to get her to relax but something was wrong. I hadn't seen her like this before and I sat with her, the nurse left us and told Liana to try and relax.

She was becoming more and more anxious and suddenly, her body slumped back on the bed, her eyes rolled back into her head and she went rigid and stopped breathing! I started screaming, 'Nurse, nurse!' I screamed so loudly it ripped a pain through my throat, and alarms started going off. The nurses came running in followed by her nephrologist who had been in her office next door. I was asked to leave the room and I just remember slumping down against the wall outside and sitting down on the floor crying my heart out: I thought she was dying.

About fifteen minutes later the nurse came out and found me still there, and said Liana was conscious again. They had taken her off dialysis and back to the ward. I had called Jay who was working in Winchester and he came straightaway. It took him a while to arrive, but once he did we were taken to a side room and it was explained that Liana seemed to have had a reaction to something whilst dialysing and that they didn't think she was doing very well at all. She was back in the ward and my Dad was sitting with her whilst we were in the meeting.

Liana was agitated and couldn't relax, she was talking total gibberish and was just vomiting and sleeping, then speaking words that didn't make sense. At one point she started to have another seizure and we were told that she needed to have a brain scan and that we could wait here for her to come back. They took her off very quickly and we waited what seemed like an eternity.

I found the hospital chapel and we spent an hour there. It was a peculiar hexagonally-shaped room with an altar and some bibles. There were some little bookmarks for sale at the door and Jay put some money in the pot and bought one that said, 'All Shall Be Well'... He passed it to me, and I still have it to this day.

I knelt quietly on the floor, begging again not to have her taken away from us. We waited outside the ward and Liana didn't come back. She had been taken to the High Dependency Unit, and a sister of the ward that we knew came to get us. I remember bursting into tears when I was told that in the scanner Liana had had an even greater seizure and that they now had had to put her onto life support.

I asked that question again, 'Is she going to die?' and the sister reassured me that they had everything under control and that we were best to go home and rest, that there was nothing we could do for her tonight.

I still had some of the large supply of sleeping tablets the doctor in Kenya had given me. When Liana had arrived at the hospital in the UK and the handover was done, they took her sleeping tablets away from her as they weren't licensed to use in the UK, so I had hidden mine away, knowing they were what kept me sane! Liana laughed at this, 'Good on you Mum,' she said as we giggled!

I took a sleeping tablet and got into bed: about an hour later at 1am the phone rang, and I was lifted quickly again to an anxious state. Liana was on life support still and had been extremely unwell. We could go down when we wanted. I didn't sleep again that night.

We arrived first thing in the morning: this was the first time that I had seen Liana on life-support, although sadly it wouldn't be the last. She was having her hair brushed and plaited by a lovely young nurse who talked to Liana as though she was awake and would have responded. This was beautiful to watch, and I was reassured that she was being looked after well.

We were asked to go for a meeting with the doctor and we met in the waiting room area. The doctor arrived with two nurses in tow: and it was explained that Liana was to have a lumbar puncture to determine what had caused this set of seizures, and that they didn't know at this stage whether any brain damage had occurred that would impair Liana's future.

Wow, that was a whole new set of worries and we anxiously waited for two days while she was kept sedated and asleep.

At this point I spent a lot of time in the chapel, private time, crying, rocking, begging again... I seemed to do lots of begging, but I was desperate.

We had been told that Liana's seizures were caused by a drug that she had been given on her return from Kenya, that was to help with her dialysing, and it seemed she had had a nasty reaction to it. As it was a drug that stayed in the system for a month, she would be on anti-seizure medication for a further two weeks until they deemed it out of her system.

They gently woke her a few days later, and we waited with anticipation to see if there was any lasting brain damage. Liana came around slowly and was very sleepy for a long time, and thankfully we felt she had all neural function as expected. It was a relief to say the least.

She was unaware of just how anxious we were, as we put on brave faces, but I would just sit in the car and cry it out when she was asleep.

She was moved to a High Dependency Unit a few days later and then back to the ward after that, when it was apparent that she was well enough. Her anxiety levels shot up again at this point and her sickness began all over again. The staff always believed it was due to stress that she was being sick; at that time I was unsure, and didn't understand how this could be happening. I argued often with them over her vomiting, and they said she couldn't go home until it stopped.

She continued to dialyse and was still losing weight. She had started to look different: and as I had never seen her so thin before, it was very concerning.

One day we were told we could take her home for a day visit. So, we arrived nice and early. It was now early December and the main aim was to get her home for Christmas. As we drove back along the road to home, sick bowls in tow, Liana was in the front passenger seat and Jay was driving. I sat in the back and realised that the sickness had stopped! Just by being away from the hospital?

We treated her gently and she spent time on the sofa. Getting up the stairs took about half an hour of one step at a time, but she really wanted to see her room, so we did it (if I remember rightly Jay carried her in the end). She was very weak and slept lots, but just to have her in our home was incredible.

Taking her back to the hospital later that evening was dreadful. She started to be sick again and I now understood what her nursing team meant. It now felt imperative to get her home to recover as soon as possible! Her team agreed, and we moved quickly, arranging her outpatient dialysis three times a week at the hospital (hospital transport was arranged for this) and we got her home!

The Pancreas Was Screwed

We had a couple of weeks at home with her resting most of the time. She was not up to many visitors, but people came and went as they could, supporting her and loving her. Everyone was devastated to see her in this way. It was a tough time on us all as a family. She was up and down emotionally and really, I think, unable to comprehend what had happened over the previous two months.

She continued her outpatients' appointments and saw her nephrology team, and we now understood that her kidney failure was permanent, and that it was hoped that she would be able to get well enough to get onto the transplant list.

We still struggled to believe this. We knew that acute kidney failure caused by pancreatitis was usually reversed within a few days, and yet we still hoped for a miracle.

Liana was still producing a small amount of urine and we took that as gold that her kidneys would kick in again. She would argue with her team at the unit that this could change, but one particularly tough outpatient appointment was an eye-opener as her nephrologist told her she had only 3% kidney function and it was going down all the time.

We howled big tears, disbelief, pain, confusion! How had any of this happened? Why did it have to happen?

It was mid-December when we struck bad luck again and woke in the middle of the night with Liana screaming out in pain. She was holding her stomach and screaming out that it was the same pain as when she was out in Africa. All hell let loose and we called 999 – (this was the second pancreatitis hit of a total of eleven to happen in the coming months) – the crew arrived and gave Liana gas and air to suck on while we headed to the local hospital.

She was in total agony: this is the part I had missed when she was in Uganda... Now it was brutal to see, and she was re-admitted to hospital as they tried to control the pain. Teams were running around, trying to get her stable again. I folded with the realisation that this was not going away.

Liana became a regular at our local A&E in the coming few months. This time she was admitted to the children's ward, which treated patients up to age twenty-three and it was more suitable for someone her age. She was continuing to vomit, perhaps now up to twenty or thirty times a day. Keeping even her medication down was a miracle and I was more and more concerned at the damage she was doing to herself.

We met some key people in our lives during this time. One of them was a lad called Jack, who had had kidney failure from birth and had received a life-saving kidney transplant at a very young age. He was a regular too, needing help with infections and related problems. I had found in his Mum a kindred spirit, someone I could be honest with and someone who knew quite a lot of answers to my millions of questions.

We also met Kayleigh, who became one of Liana's best friends over the next few years. I am certain

Kayleigh's Mum could write her own book about Kayleigh, who in Liana's name became a staunch advocate for organ donation and who sadly passed away in a tragic skiing accident fourteen months after we lost Liana. You couldn't make the story up.

Kayleigh and Liana became inseparable and were a pair of energetic lunatics, always having fun and making the best of their hospital stays together. They were both regulars on the ward over the coming weeks, looking after each other.

So, as Liana stayed in our local hospital, she was taken to Dorchester by hospital transport for her thrice weekly dialysis sessions.

It was becoming increasingly likely that she would be in hospital for Christmas, but we did some bargaining on Christmas Eve with a young doctor, whom we managed to wrap around our little fingers, and he signed her out on an overnight release at 6pm...

That night, I had both my girls back under the same roof again and the regular early night with new Christmas pyjamas filled my heart with total joy. Liana woke up at home on Christmas morning! Nothing else mattered. But she was sick and weak and could stay awake for barely half an hour at a time.

We sat together on Christmas morning, opening gifts, watching Liana fall asleep, waking her up, opening more gifts, watching her fall asleep... You will appreciate how long it took to get through the presents!

It seemed not even Christmas lunch was going to happen that day, either. I was standing in the kitchen, turkey in one hand, cloths in the other, cleaning up yet another round of sickness. Except this time there was blood in it, too.

So anxious was I by the vomiting I couldn't prevent myself from bursting into tears. I just longed for a normal Christmas. I put Caitlin in the car to drop her at her Dad's, left Jay alone with the turkey, and Liana and I went back to hospital. It was agony for her, I could see that, but I was totally exhausted too, mentally and physically. I would have said at that time that it was the worst Christmas I have ever had, but there was worse to come the next year...

Continuum

January 2011: The New Year didn't bring much joy. We finally got Liana well enough to come home again, and she was still being collected for dialysis at Dorchester hospital three times a week. It was snowing quite hard, as I watched her leave the house to get in the hospital transport car. This day she had to walk down to the bottom of our road as the car couldn't get up it due to the ice. I watched at 6am in the dark as she walked down the hill and thought to myself how tiny and fragile she looked now, her coat was huge on her and it made me sad. She looked pathetic and it burned at my heart.

I had gone back to bed to sleep for a bit, and about an hour later Liana rang my mobile; this time she was different, in her voice, and she said to me, 'Mum, I don't have to dialyse, my kidneys are starting to work again as my bloods are so good!' and she started to cry with joy! I leapt up out of bed and was happy for the first time in weeks! This was amazing news. 'I can come home,' she cried. It was totally overwhelming, and our minds raced, and we were in total shock at this news.

Liana was brought home by her hospital car and she looked relaxed and happy for the first time in what was now months – we couldn't believe our ears at the news...

The hospital rang at 10.30am that morning and Liana was told, in a cruel blow, that the on-duty doctor that morning had read the wrong results for her bloodwork; he had read the end of session results from last time, and that an error had been made: she did have to dialyse, and her kidneys were still gone... It was an awful throwback into the depression that she had felt, and I couldn't believe that some idiot could have done that to her. It was painful... she went to bed, didn't want to talk to anyone and slept for the rest of the day.

The pain and the vomiting persisted throughout the early part of that year. At one point Liana was taken back into A&E in acute pain. While waiting to see a doctor she had an allergic reaction to the drug she was given, and was rushed into the Resuscitation Unit.

I was shaken, and the anxiety washed over me again as they worked on her, and I was asked to wait outside while they treated her. I was panic-stricken once again... Eventually she was moved to the ward and she was insistent that it was the same pain as when she was in Africa, but the doctor told her that this wasn't possible as she had had acute pancreatitis at that time and it doesn't continue if it is acute.

She thought she was going mad: she knew her pain, and insisted it was pancreatitis again. She was dreadfully unwell and was heavily sedated with pain relief.

It was then discovered through scans that she had a large pancreatic pseudocyst. It was the size of an orange and was hanging down from the back of the pancreas, and was a collection of fluid that had built up due to the damage in the pancreas. It was decided that she needed an operation to cut this out (resection), and she was sent to the BRI (Bristol Royal Infirmary) for treatment.

As we arrived in the ambulance, Liana was met by a top surgeon who explained that they needed to make a tunnel from the pseudocyst and route it into the back of her stomach. They couldn't remove it as it would just form again due to the damage on her pancreas, so they would allow it to continually flow through her stomach to keep it drained. Her operation would be the next morning, once they had stabilised her bloods with dialysis and were then happy to move forward. In the meantime she was to have some fluid aspirated (drained) from the cyst, and she was taken down for this procedure immediately.

Sedated, she was wheeled off to the day surgery room while I waited outside. They inserted a tube down her throat and into her stomach and pushed through a needle to aspirate what they could, until the needle blocked. They found lots of debris in the fluid, but it was amylase, as they had expected, and they were happy to go ahead with her operation the next day.

She didn't remember that she had been thrashing around heavily while sedated, and the doctor took a right hook at one point, I think...

I stayed at a hotel locally and we were up at the crack of dawn for her operation. She was to recover in ICU and that is where I met her a few hours later. She was heavily sedated, and the operation had gone well. She had a nasal vacuum tube into her stomach, which was drawing out all the fluid that was being released, and it was coming out thick and fast. She had pain, but it was being well controlled by the team. Her pancreas had been damaged so much in the first instance of pancreatitis in Uganda that this was another complication.

A few days later, she was allowed a few spoonsful of soup and then was horrified when this started to pour out of the drain too. The nurse had forgotten to turn off the vacuum, so Liana got the taste, but it ran out of her tummy as fast as it could be pumped... She was not impressed. I laughed, which annoyed her even more; nothing was funny at this point for her.

I was with her from dawn to dusk, only ever going home to get clean clothes and see Caitlin for a few hours. Caitlin and Jay visited when they could, but Liana was in a dark place during these days and couldn't be lifted. Her vomiting had taken over and it became very clear to us all now it was a mental health problem. It was so frustrating to watch, but no amount of talking could calm her, as she was extremely fraught.

We had gone through her GP to ask for mental health assistance, but sadly Liana's application had been declined as it was deemed she wasn't sick enough... I was unsure how sick you had to be?

The hospital ward she was moved to after ICU was very old and dark with small narrow windows: it reminded me of a prison. She didn't speak a whole lot at that time, just slept and threw up. I persuaded her one day to come for a walk with me and she left the building in a wheelchair. We sat on a patch of grass we found in the city centre. I left her there and ran across the road to a shop to buy us both ice lollies: she closed her eyes in the sunshine and soaked it up for a while.

I thought how pale she looked; she was now about six stone in weight, and although only 5ft 1ins, she looked almost deathly: it was hard to see. She couldn't eat for fear of her pancreas 'going off' again and was so mentally unwell that she would just vomit anyway. It was like a type of anorexia, although she wasn't worried about her appearance and weight at all.

It became all too apparent that she was scared to death of what had happened over the last few months. I came to the conclusion that she was suffering from a version of PTSD (Post-Traumatic Stress Disorder), except that she was still in the wars, which fuelled her ongoing anxiety.

I wish I had known how to deal with her mental health: in fact it is what she eventually went through that allows me now to understand so much more. Too little too late maybe, I paid privately for her to see a psychologist, as it was clear that she needed help: and our local NHS service couldn't give her the care she needed, as their resources were too stretched.

After a few days on the ward at the BRI, a problem struck again, and she was found to be holding fluid in her chest cavity behind her lungs, which it seemed was a complication of her operation. It was affecting her breathing, so she needed to have the fluid aspirated as soon as possible. The doctor hid his instruments from Liana until she was looking away. The needle he was going to insert into her back to drain the fluid was so long I thought it would pierce right through to the other side of her!

A whole heap of fluid was drained, and it helped her breathing enormously. I could have easily passed out at this stage. When she finally got a look at the needle, her eyes widened like pancakes. After uttering the f-word, she settled back down. We laughed at the whole situation: it seemed that everything that could happen was happening and it was almost laughable, the relentlessness of it all.

At around this time, Liana was transferred back to our local hospital for recuperation and we heard from the doctors that all testing for tropical diseases had now come back clear. Genetic testing had also been done and showed that Liana was a carrier of one of the Cystic Fibrosis genes, though this was not what had caused her initial problem. It was now thought that the only feasible cause for this was an adverse reaction to the anti-malaria tablets she was taking in Uganda.

She was advised against taking Malarone as there is a family history of depression, so was given Doxycycline and started taking it a week before she left for Uganda. It was a daily dose and would be taken for the duration of her stay abroad and for a while after as a precaution. Of course, now the two nosebleeds that Liana had had, in that week before she left, may have been for a reason. We had thought that it was just the stress/nerves of leaving home, but perhaps the chaos in her system was already starting?

Back at our local hospital, Liana was well known by the staff and had a little side room of her own, as her constant diarrhoea was an infection threat to others. She was still losing weight and passing hideous poo (I was going to write bowel movements, but Liana would have said poo or worse!). Further tests had been done and it was now deemed that she had no digestive ability due to the damage to her pancreas, so she started taking Creon, a digestive enzyme capsule treatment usually used by those with CF (Cystic Fibrosis) and of course by those who had such pancreatic damage that they couldn't produce the amylase needed – this explained so much, and she was told that she would eventually learn exactly how many tablets she would need at each meal; for example a biscuit might require one tablet while a meal would need four to six, depending on the fat content. If she didn't take enough tablets she would have an upset tummy, and she needed to eat a healthier diet to help with this, but that was rarely in Liana's remit and she would eat what she could around her renal diet and a little bit more...

Her Grandad had come to visit from the USA which made her face light up. She was in desperate need of something to make her happy and forget her ills and this visit did just that.

We managed to get a day release from the hospital and spent the day at the beach at Lyme Regis. Jay carried Liana on his back down the steep hill to the beach as she had zero energy to walk and we sat, shaded from the hot sun, and tried to relax just for a little while.

Back at home later that day, we were sitting in the garden laughing at how sunburned Grandad's head was (and how much trouble he would be in when he got back to his lovely wife in America!) and I made some food for us all, just a picnic style tea. There must have been something good in that sea air that day as Liana grabbed a roll filled with cheese and ate it with passion, a move we hadn't seen in months. 'I just want to eat it Mum,' she said, almost in tears, and she scoffed it down and wasn't sick! She knew her sickness was emotionally driven, and she was trying with all her might to fight back.

She had finally relaxed: the sun, seeing Grandad, the sea air, I don't know; but I didn't question it, I just enjoyed it...

We went back to the hospital later that evening and she was exhausted and settled back into her familiar routine.

Her dialysis care had been moved to Southmead hospital in Bristol by now: her new surgeon had taken over her care in the hope of moving her dialysis sessions to the local centre in Yeovil. This happened, and Liana joined in there on Monday, Wednesday and Friday evenings. These times suited her better as she could go straight to bed and sleep after each session, and not feel sick or wiped out for the rest of the day.

I guess some people feel better after dialysis, but sadly Liana wasn't one of those people. I am sure that some of this was her mental attitude towards the realisation that she was always going to need dialysis or treatment of some kind. I can say this now, as we realised later that the kidney transplant wasn't the 'cure' we thought it would be; it is simply another form of treatment that needs constant monitoring and tablet adjustment... Dialysis is on the cards at any time if the kidney is rejected or fails naturally.

It was around this time that she had a renal fistula placed in her left arm, just above the elbow, to replace the catheter used for haemodialysis (blood filtering).

With most dialysis catheters, a cuff is placed under the skin to help hold the catheter in place. The blood flow rate from the catheter to the dialyser may not be as fast as for other forms of access to the bloodstream (i.e. an Arteriovenous or AV graft or fistula); which might have resulted in her blood not being cleaned thoroughly, a possible explanation for Liana constantly feeling sick and heady with no ability to concentrate, even after dialysis. She had suffered with an infection in the catheter and had had a replacement, which she found painful and frightening.

Catheters have a greater tendency to become infected than the other access types because the device is both inside and outside the body. A catheter must always be kept clean and dry; swimming or bathing is usually restricted. Getting dressed may disturb the catheter at the exit site, so care needs to be taken. It was a total nightmare, so I understand why she was to have a fistula, except it was another realisation that her kidneys would never function again and we both hated what it meant.

An Arteriovenous (AV) fistula used for haemodialysis is a direct connection of an artery to a vein. Once the fistula is created it is a natural part of the body. This is the preferred type of access because once the fistula properly matures and gets bigger and stronger, it provides an access with good blood flow that can last for decades. After the fistula is surgically created, it can take weeks to months before the fistula matures and is ready to be used for haemodialysis. Liana was given exercises to do with a little squeezy ball to strengthen the area, which worked well; and she had to be extremely careful not to do any damage to the arm, so that the fistula would grow strong. Once ready for use, the catheter could be removed and two huge needles would be inserted each time she dialysed.

This didn't go down well with her at all. She appreciated the reasons for the change, but the needles were intimidating and they hurt. She dragged her feet, struggled to deal with the emotions yet again; and would cry and often become obnoxious with the nurses as they inserted the 'javelins' (as she called them). It's ironic to think that one day she would insert her own needles into her arm for dialysis.

I don't ever remember a time that she 'settled' into her dialysis routine: it was always awful for her, and she was often so anxious at the dialysis centre that she was rude or in tears and generally unable to cope. I would sit with her, or a friend would go, but it didn't help much when she felt so rough, so incredibly ill. She had so many other problems that it seemed that dialysis just accentuated them. The care given to her was wonderful though, and she became close to some of the lovely nurses at the dialysis centre in our home town.

As a regular, she got to know some other patients. She came home sobbing one evening as someone had died at the centre. It was too close for comfort. She knew she couldn't dialyse forever without complications, and this sad turn of events had made her all too aware of this.

Blue Lights and London

That summer nearly a year on from her departure for Uganda saw another four painful admissions to hospital.

Seeing her scream in pain from the acute discomfort in her pancreas was just evil. There seemed to be no end to the pain she suffered during that summer of 2011. She would clutch her stomach and writhe around, unable to bear it. When her pain became overwhelming, we would summon an ambulance and spent many days sitting in the hospital's A&E department side unit waiting for another admission. It was relentless. Only when she had been drugged up to the eyeballs did the pain recede a little.

The ambulance staff got to know her very well, as did the gastro team. Lots of junior doctors were brought round to see Liana and to be told her story so that they could learn new things, I guess. Liana got to know them all and they often stopped and chatted for a while, which was kind. Although the hospital staff were probably as fed up with her as we were with having to take her there, people were so friendly: the porters, the receptionists, the teams who worked on her. All felt sympthy for this frail little thing enduring so much at such a young age.

She was repeatedly told by our local hospital that it couldn't be chronic pancreatitis, even though she knew the pain was the same as it had been before.

She turned out to be right ... I wish people had listened to her.

In August, Liana (a little stronger and wanting independence) drove herself up to Southmead Hospital for her regular renal check-up. My best friend Manda had gone with her as I had to try and catch up with my publishing job. Manda called me on the way, to say that they had stopped the car just short of Bristol as Li had some tummy pain and was running a temperature, but that they were going to continue with the journey and would call me later.

When Manda called later, Liana had been admitted as an in-patient and they believed that she was having another attack of pancreatitis. I jumped in my car and shot to Bristol with speed. Anxiety always washed over me on those journeys, never sure of what state she was going to be in when I got there. She was in agony, screaming out in pain again. Having been given some super strong pain relief, she was taken to a ward and stayed for another ten days.

It was decided during this time that she needed to be moved to a specialist care unit in London, under a team of hepatobiliary specialists, as not only her pancreas was playing up, but her liver function tests were now not where they should be.

It took a few days to get her a place in London, but with a lot of hard work the medical team were successful and, in the September of that year, an ambulance took her to University College Hospital London (UCLH) on the Euston Road.

I was to travel up the next day, and knew I would find Liana very nervous in this new environment.

It seemed as though being in a London hospital signalled to us that she was really seriously ill; except of course she had been *seriously ill* for nearly a year already.

Arrangements had been made for her to dialyse at the Royal Free Hospital in Hampstead, North London as UCLH didn't have a renal department. She was transported by ambulance three times a week to keep her up to date with her dialysis needs.

It became quickly apparent that the team in London had no hesitation in prescribing powerful medications. If you had to be ill, this was the place to be.

After more tests, it was decided that she needed to have a stent placed in the neck of her pancreas. The tissue was so damaged that she was continually afflicted with pancreatitis because the digestive enzymes were unable to escape into the digestive tract (which is normal). This meant that the enzymes were eating away at the pancreas itself. Surgery was planned for when she was strong enough.

But she wasn't strong enough, and was going downhill regarding her pain; the team were unable to give her the required pain medications without filtration (which is a gentle but continuous twenty-four hourly form of dialysis that would keep the toxins from building up), and the decision was made to put her back onto life support in the ICU.

It felt like a massive backwards jump, as she had been in London for a couple of weeks at this stage, and again I found myself back in a hospital chapel. A volunteer called Rose would want to chat for ages, but I would eventually get some quiet time and pray over and over, for fear that I had missed out something vital which might mean that my prayer hadn't been heard.

I went back to Somerset for the odd night to see Caitlin and pick up some clean clothes, but only when I could get someone else to take over the visit. Friends and family did this, but it was very hard for most of them to get to London and spend time there.

I was lucky enough to be able to stay with Jay's sister in Surrey. Normally I would get back at 10pm and leave first thing, often at 8am to get back on the train to central London. I became a professional at the underground system and always found the cheapest way I could, as I had already racked up a huge amount of debt to be with her. Sadly, as Liana was an adult, there were no facilities for me to stay with her overnight. I was exceptionally lucky that Jay was still able to work and that my boss was flexible about my working hours. He still paid me even though I was self-employed whilst working in his publishing firm. We had established a super relationship years before; and it is people like that who don't ever realise just how much they help you.

The operation for her pancreatic stent went ahead a few days after the team in ICU had been able to take her off life-support. Her pain was less, and she was able to go back to the Royal Free for dialysis. It was a relatively short operation and I met her in the recovery room. The doctor wasn't very happy with how things had gone, and he said that they did have the stent in place but that it was incredibly hard for him to access the area due to damage to the tissue and that we might have future problems.

He was right: about ten days later she was screaming in pain again, and the pancreas had started to go off like a firework factory again: the scans showed no sign of the stent, so it had managed to dislodge, and pass. This was possibly the tenth time she had had pancreatitis during this year, as the organ was so severely damaged, and she went back into the ICU. Their care was marvellous, but it was incredibly hard.

The main concern at this point was that the hospital felt that they were unable to get Liana to the stage she would even be able to have the very much needed kidney transplant. An MDT (multi-disciplinary team) meeting was held and I was invited in to discuss options.

I had never considered that someone could not be well enough for a transplant, but this was our reality! I felt the whole room spin around me and I left to go and get some fresh air. I called home, my parents, and Liana's wider family to try and digest what I had been told. It might be that Liana lived out her life in hospital... I wasn't prepared for this. This wasn't part of my deal with God or with her!

They waited another week, and one of the consultants decided that he would take on the job of trying again to get a stent into the pancreas. It failed, and he came out of theatre looking totally lost, and deeply upset that even with his considerable skills he was unable to breach the scar tissue and damage. He said that he was sorry; He had never been unable to do this operation and he felt he had let Liana down, but he had done his very best, and I did all that I could to reassure him. What a wonderful man.

Liana started to get weaker from all the operations and medicines. Travelling to dialysis was becoming a risk and was very painful for her. At a loss, the team had decided that there was not a lot else that they could do for her.

The Prof

One day, Liana was strong enough to be wheeled down to the chapel herself. She was at an extremely low ebb and cried for most of the time she was there. We sat in silence and said prayers – I could see the look of desperation on her face, as she was wondering just how much more she could take. Then the ground started to rumble and vibrate and there was a low thunder-like noise and she shrieked, as if she was witnessing some divine intervention; had her prayers been heard? No, it was a tube train under us and we both howled with laughter at the look on her face!

Our hero came in the form of Professor Massimo Malago, a specialist in hepatobiliary-pancreatic, oncologic and transplantation surgery. The Prof (as we came to call him) had offered to help Liana and do the operation that nobody else wanted to do – a pancreatojejunostomy...

Wiki description: (longitudinal) pancreaticojejunostomy (LPJ) consists of a longitudinal incision of the pancreatic duct and implantation of the tail of the gland into the Roux-en-Y limb of the jejunum (middle bowel) following splenectomy and distal pancreatectomy.

Yep, that's all... oh, and to transplant the liver bile duct into a piece of the bowel too, as it was partially blocked.

Liana was transferred to the care of the Prof, and eventually moved to the Royal Free (another five stops for me on the Northern Line every day!). Once again she was given incredible care and got to know all the staff. She was now able to go just 'upstairs' for dialysis instead of needing an hour in an ambulance through the streets of London and, as Liana informed me, 'They deal in hard drugs here', so that her pain needs were thoroughly met!

She was still vomiting lots each day, but I noticed this slowed a little as she felt safer with the Prof at her side. We were able to venture outside into the sun as she got stronger, ready for the big operation. We would wander slowly to the end of the road and sit and watch the busy London traffic. We walked on one occasion to a local park and just sat and watched the world go by.

She was sent home on the 12th December (a few weeks later) to get ready for this next procedure. It was a huge operation and she needed to be ready both physically and mentally. We enjoyed a few days of sofa and bed rest, dialysing locally and being able to see friends and loved ones. On the morning of the 18th she was collected, to have twenty-four hours to stabilise her dialysis bloods and to be in the right place medically for the surgery.

Jay and I followed her up to London and spent a few hours with her that evening. We stayed in a local hotel so that we could be with her at 7am as she went down for surgery. It was an early start and she was clearly nervous. A friend she had met in the hospital had visited her the previous evening and given her a little white Christmas tree. We knew that she would be sent straight to the ICU after her operation, so we gathered up her few belongings for later.

The Prof came and spoke with her and told her very clearly, 'I am going to do exactly what I need to do, Liana, to keep you alive, but I need to know that you are ready to take the next step with me, because you are the one who has to do the bit after me and deal with the pain and the recuperation, and this will be harder than anything that you have done so far'... She promised him that she was up for it and we all believed her. She was ready to fight this battle and get her body ready for transplant.

We walked up and down hospital corridors, slept in our car in the car park (which cost nearly as much as the hotel to park in!) and we even ventured down Oxford Street just to try and break up the day. There was no news as we arrived back at the hospital at 5pm and, having said our goodbyes at the theatre entrance at 8am, we had been hoping to have her back with us by now. We loitered and got anxious. I couldn't stand still, and thought that perhaps she could not cope with such a tough operation, as she was down to about five stone in weight and it seemed that she might have been too weak...

It was 9.45pm by the time the Prof walked down to where we were sitting on the corridor floor outside the recovery unit. He smelled amazing (Liana told him this on many occasions) even then, as he wrapped his arms around 'the Mamma' as he called me. In his thick Italian accent, he told us that he had somehow done what he had planned to do but that Liana's case had presented him with many problems.

Areas of total devastation inside her: a pancreas that was hardly recognisable, from which he had had to remove two thirds as it was so malformed. The head of the pancreas had been cored like an apple and then cut open, butterflied, and linked to a piece of her bowel so that the enzymes would drain away into her bowel and not get blocked in the pancreas. There was not much pancreas left at all but he hoped that she would stay off insulin for a time.

He had also found so much damage to her liver bile duct that he had transplanted that away from the biliary area and into the bowel, also. We could kiss her goodnight, but she was not to be woken by them until the next day when they were certain they could stabilise her in the ICU. She looked so vulnerable, on life-support, and so small and fragile. But she had come so far, I had to believe she could do this.

Of course, we didn't sleep much back at Jay's sister's house. I hadn't wanted to leave the hospital at all... When I finally slept it was only for a couple of hours and I dragged Jay out of bed at a ridiculous time to drive me back to the hospital in North London. I called ahead and enquired about Liana and how her night had been, but they said that they had been unable to wake her and that she wasn't playing ball. The doctor would be coming in to see her soon. I made Jay drive faster. In fact, I wouldn't even let him park the car: I insisted he drop me off at the door and let me run up, and he could follow on behind.

I raced up to the ICU and got buzzed in: I knew the drill and walked past her bed to the sink unit to put on an apron and wash my hands. About turn, and I looked across at her bed and she was sitting up taking a sip of water from a straw! Jesus, child! Don't do that to me!

I was crying tears of relief and just held her tight. She looked tiny and fragile in the hospital bed and was covered again in pipes and wires. This time she had a tube in one nostril for feeding (once she was well enough to have liquid food directly into her bowel, bypassing the healing area) and a tube in the other nostril for draining from her stomach in the meantime, so that the operation site could heal.

She had 48 staples across her tummy from left to right. She looked as though she had been split across the middle and she dozed and slept for the next few days.

Of course, we knew Christmas this year would be in hospital, and we prayed she could get out of ICU before then, so we could have time alone as a family. She was unable to have the hoped-for spinal block to help with her pain due to having blood thinners, and so this was a particularly agonising time for her. But she knew that this was what the Prof had meant when he had asked her if she was prepared to play her part.

The team all stood around her bed trying to find a solution to her screaming out in pain; they had given her so many drugs and needed to find something to help. As I came through to her bed after a quick tea break, she was crying and wailing and really panicking about the fact that she could hear what they were saying through the curtains around her bed, and that they were unable to give her other drugs as the risks were too high. She was shouting at a doctor – there were about six of them surrounding her bed - and she was being rude and obnoxious, telling them that they weren't helping her. She was totally petrified and unable to be rational. I hadn't seen her in so much pain before.

The ICU sister was trying to get Liana to calm down, but it was all too much and so I used my maternal instinct as her mother, and stood in front of her and told her to look at my eyes. I asked her, 'Do you trust me?' She said that she did... I asked her, 'Do you remember what the Prof said to you about your part of the deal?" She said that she did... 'So ' I said, 'every single person here around your bed is here to do one thing, and that is to keep you alive, to not take any risks with your health and to get you onto that transplant list, do you hear me? They don't WANT you to be in pain, but they cannot perform bloody miracles and are trying with everything they have. Now, you will calm down and help yourself by working with them, and will listen to them!'

She did: I felt incredibly proud... The ICU sister opened her eyes wide at me and just looked at me as though to say, 'Thank God you took control of the situation because we didn't have it' – which are exactly the words she used to me later that day when we had a moment together.

I always reminded Liana, that it doesn't matter how sick you are or how scared you are, you NEVER speak to anyone like that again, not me, not them. She didn't... she understood this is what the Prof meant. This was the bit she had to do, he warned her: he meant business.

So, on Christmas Eve we managed to get her into a private room on the recovery ward of the gastro team. Liana was a sight for sore eyes, still wired up to endless monitors and drips, covered in scars and bruises, but we had made it out of the ICU. She was still in a dangerous position medically but was as stable as could be expected. Jay went home to collect Caitlin and we three booked into the hotel on the corner for Christmas Eve. We left Liana to sleep in the evening, and the three of us went to a Chinese restaurant for a little food and rest and to try and give Caitlin some semblance of normal life in this chaotic and scary time.

We exchanged our own gifts that night in our hotel room and woke at the crack of dawn to be with Liana. We took in heaps of gifts. We tried to be happy, but it was a miserable day really. Poor Caitlin was as brave as she could be, and Liana managed only to open one gift before going back to sleep, then another gift, another sleep: everything was just too much.

Caitlin and I went to get some food at lunchtime from the cafeteria; Jay didn't eat much that day, and I burst into tears at the feeling I was letting Caitlin down: she was suffering through this too, and it was a stark reminder of how the whole family was being ripped apart during this dreadful time. We sat on hard orange plastic chairs all day watching Liana sleep, wake briefly and then sleep again. She was still being sick and had terrible tummy pains and was still very unwell. Like a little kitten, sitting there in her bed.

Jay took Caitlin and me home that night, so that Caitlin could go and spend some time with her Dad and his family, and I could refresh my suitcase and get back to the hospital the next day. I hated being away from them all, and cried often.

Everyone was doing all they could all the time, but life had to go on and I generally felt totally alone with it all. Friends and family had to work and look after their own lives and it seemed that life really was going on for everyone else. I saw people rarely, and it was a very low time for us all. I just wanted my family at home under the same roof. I wanted us all to be together and for all this shit to go away. It was all a bit surreal.

So, of course, never one to go gently, Liana had now managed to pick up a hospital bug, C-Diff! She became very unwell with it (she must have been exceptionally unwell to allow her sister to change her bed-pans as she had no bowel control at all) and it became severe infected C-Diff, just incredibly painful and potentially life-threatening!

She was given more drugs to help combat this and her heart rate was sky high; dangerously so for a few hours, and doctors were rushed to her side. She was briefly back in the ICU for a few days and became seriously ill, but as it was brought under control she managed to get into her own room again in time for the NYE celebrations, and she 'bagged a room' (her words not mine) which was south-facing so that she could see the London Eye as the fireworks went off! There had to be a bonus for her somewhere!

I had gone home for New Year's Eve as she had settled and was able to relax a little. She had managed to have her staples, all forty-eight, removed from across her tummy just before New Year and was a little chattier.

Well, it seems that while the Mamma is away, the children will play, and her lovely friend Ani (who had been a hospital buddy at UCLH and a seasoned hospital attendee herself) had come to visit late at night as she was in London for NYE, and had got Liana in a wheelchair and taken her outside to the M&S food hall next door to the hospital... after midnight!! Oh, dear Lord! I was sure this wasn't allowed, and I guess nobody ever found out, but the girls laughed as they told me! They were told off (by me) but I secretly smiled that Liana had had just a small amount of normal, naughty girls' fun!

Then, in good old Liana fashion, she was at home on January 6th, lying on the sofa, able to recuperate at home! Extremely weak and being tube fed again, but able to eat small meals and take it slowly, very slowly. I was unsure how she had gone from being told she'd be having a month in hospital post-op, to being home within three weeks: she was remarkable.

We had many trips to see the Prof and he gave Liana his mobile phone number and told her, 'You need me, you ring me' and that was how it was, that spring.

She needed him quite often: there were complications, as expected, and she would be taken back to London for checks and scans and the occasional stay due to pain from scar adhesions. She was starting to be sick a little less, as she gained emotional strength from the knowledge that her pancreas couldn't kick off any more: it had been in the hands of the Prof, and that was enough for her.

Two incredible things happened that spring: the first one on May 8th 2012. She finally became well enough to join the transplant list! This brought many tears of joy, and her team at Southmead Hospital in Bristol made her fully aware of what this meant.

We had discussed with them a double transplant of kidney and pancreas, but after much thought and conversation she decided to just go for a kidney as there was still a little pancreas function left at that time, she wasn't yet diabetic, and the recovery from a double transplant was much harder.

It would have put her further towards the top of the list, but she made that decision. She felt that if the average pancreas lasted for six years after transplant, then she could potentially be coming up to thirty and already needing another one, so it was an informed decision. As always, the support she received from her transplant clinic was incredible.

There were rules: she was always to be within a couple of hours of her transplant hospital and be contactable twenty-four hours a day. She knew the odds, and the average wait time based on her age and circumstances was eight years. This gnawed at her, but we tried to believe that it could be at any moment and that the day would one day come, and only when it was right.

The second incredible thing to happen was that Liana, having been nominated during the previous year, was to be a torchbearer in the Olympic torch relay! So, after much excited waiting on 22nd May 2012, day four of the Torch's route through the UK, we got up at the crack of dawn and all assembled with the other torchbearers in our hometown.

We left her on the Olympic bus that went around the UK, and she was incredibly honoured and excited. She had paid her £200 to get to keep the torch she carried and off they went to get dropped off at their various points. We were stationed at the end of her finishing her relay so that she could join her family after her part, and my parents and other family went up to the section from where she was to start.

She was number ten of that day, with a time slot assigned of 7.39am. Like the other participants, she had to run 300m but of course, she was too sick to run anywhere so she walked (and apparently too slowly, ha-ha), and was guided by the volunteers on the relay up over the hill where we first caught sight of her.

How ironic that she walked the torch past the hospital that had been her home so many times in the last eighteen months... She held the torch aloft as though it was the greatest moment of her life, and it possibly was up to that point. The crowd cheered her and we all cried with joy and disbelief that this moment had ever been possible.

The grin on her face was so wide and she came down over the hill looking like the cat who'd got the cream. The crowds were cheering and whooping, it was a hive of excitement and she came to join a fellow torchbearer called Amy, who was taking the flame from Liana. They stood together for a moment, having met on the bus only that morning. Liana's story had captured them all during their time together, so they exchanged the flame by linking their torches and Amy hugged Liana tightly before setting off herself.

The flame was put out on Liana's torch and we all ran to greet her and to hug her quickly before she had to get onto the Olympic bus and follow the route of the flame. We had been told we could pick her up an hour later at the drop off point, with her torch. This we did, and then we all as a family, and friends, went to have breakfast at a local pub in town where Liana drew much attention with her torch as she shared the moment with us all.

Later that day, exhausted but elated, Liana took the torch up to the hospital ward that had cared for her and proudly allowed many to hold it and admire it. She then went over to her old school in Sherborne and showed it off in an assembly, much to the delight of many of her old teachers and all the pupils. She basked in the glory of being a torchbearer for a very long time, and later even had a tattoo saying 'Torchbearer' written beautifully in ink across her side.

Live Life Give Life

Over that summer and the winter that followed, Liana tried to gain back a little independence. She was getting some mental health care privately and was doing everything in her power to recoup some strength. She was eating, and still dialysing three times a week. She was often at the hospital in London for regular check-ups with the Prof, and suffered a lot from scars internally as the operation had been so huge. Pain was still an issue for her but not as crippling as it had been.

It was a struggle to do much, so Liana decided to go back to college and study for a while. She had always wanted to join the police force but now that it wasn't possible, she decided to study law and to see how she could develop that area. The college were incredibly supportive of her and put plans in place to assist her. They gave her flexible learning and a room to lie down in, should she need a rest or medication during the day. She had a disabled parking space at the entrance and a good relationship with the staff.

Caitlin was already at the college, so I knew that Liana wasn't alone if she became sick, but I expect Caitlin found her a pain in the ass at the best of times. It was while Liana was at college one day that I received a phone call from her, crying heavily down the phone: I raced in, and I found her in an office, being supported. It had been because her close friend at dialysis, Graham, had passed away.

He was much older than Liana, in his fifties and riddled with cancer. He knew he was not getting better and still smoked like a trooper. He would often drive Liana home from dialysis after their joint shift, when her hospital taxi was going to be delayed and to save her from waiting. He was able to talk to Liana and she to him; they cursed a lot about their situation and they shared a huge fondness for each other. She had visited him, and they had eaten dinner together and she nagged him about taking his tablets and looking after himself: he didn't listen, but she loved him dearly.

His death was a huge blow for her, not just the loss of a friend but the whole 'death thing' becoming real. She didn't want to deal with that at such a young age, but it was all around her.

She had previously seen people have heart attacks and even someone who died whilst on dialysis in the room she was in. It was another layer of pain and emotion that she shouldn't have to have had, but she couldn't choose it, it was going to happen, and much too often it seemed.

We had Christmas 2012 together at home... It was a lovely day, emotional but lovely. There were of course strains; we had come through two years of total hell and she was still emotionally unwell, depressed I guess, and even the term PTSD had been thrown about a little. I could understand that: a life-changing illness in the middle of Uganda at the age of eighteen could do that. She was easily snappy and could cause a row, but I suppose that made us a normal family again.

The New Year brought fresh hope for us all. 2013 gave Liana a few visits to hospital, with many acute admissions that could be dealt with using pain relief and a change of medication. Each visit just as tough as the one before.

She struggled to keep to her strict diet as she had a love of food and wanted to eat everything she couldn't. Her bowel couldn't handle this for two reasons: mainly due to the restriction it faced from being cut about so much and because often she would have a bowel obstruction and be taken into hospital whilst it cleared or until she vomited it up; and secondly because she had no digestive ability, and trying to get her dose of digestive enzymes right was a nightmare; so it was either not staying in her system very long at all, or making her very bloated and ill... Nothing was easy.

Liana studied as much as she could that year, mostly at home. Dialysis became even tougher for her mentally, the longer it went on. She had a lot of anger that she should have to do this when she wanted to be out there living the life her friends were enjoying. At the same time she was conflicted because she was aware that others suffered more.

She became an advocate for Live Life Give Life, an organ donation charity, and became involved in several events locally and as far away as Exeter and Bristol. She made lots of new friends, all able to understand what she was going through. They were all part of a group they hadn't chosen to join, able to empathise with each other's pain and fears.

She had tried to hold down a part-time job in a local pub but had found it too physically difficult, and sadly had to resign and then resort to applying for Disability Living Allowance benefit. When she first came back from Africa she had refused to claim as she felt it was wrong, even though many had encouraged her to do it to be able to support herself. She still didn't feel right about it, so when she was left with no option it didn't come easy.

She had a disability badge for her car as she couldn't walk a long distance. This always caused her problems, and, on occasions, she was challenged by someone who felt she didn't look disabled.

Many times, she was made to cry by the bullying behaviour of other motorists and would arrive home upset screaming 'why me?'. Sometimes she would fight back and once got back in her car and followed a woman home who had yelled at her: 'People like you mean real disabled people cannot park!' Liana was so upset that she knocked on her door and proceeded to tell her exactly how and why she was disabled and what she had gone through. The lady was so apologetic that she cried as she listened to her story. They became friends... Funny how things like that happen!

Stories like that made me mad, they made me cry. Wasn't she going through enough without idiots being nasty too?! I can't say that I didn't hate the world back then, because I did; she was my little girl and I wanted to stop this happening to her, except that I couldn't.

With just a few more hospital stays that year, Liana finally managed to pass her Law exam with a B grade! She was delighted, but thought that she could have got an A had she not been so sick and off college for so much of the time... Never satisfied!

Through contacts at the college she had started to mentor a couple of teenagers in our town. It enabled her to help others who were perhaps suffering or needed guidance, and I know that she personally arranged some horse riding for one of the girls and would take her out on a drive to the coast, etc. I was proud of her for doing this; and on the few occasions that she was well enough, I know she always made a positive impact.

...

April 28th 2013 was a day to remember. Liana had been accompanied into town by a friend of hers for a mooch around, and I got a frantic phone call; she was crying, and I could hear her shaking: she had received a call from her transplant co-ordinator telling her that she had the chance of a kidney transplant!

She was second on the list for this call but there was a chance that the priority patient could fail their last-minute tests, so she was to treat it as an urgent call. She was the 'back-up' this time, but it was a chance we were going to take, and action stations started! She was too shaky to drive home so her friend brought her, and they abandoned her car in town. In the five minutes it had taken them to get home from town I had gathered together all her necessaries and we left immediately.

We decided to take the main motorway to the hospital as the A roads into Bristol were often clogged. About ten miles towards the end of our journey up the M5 we were greeted by standstill traffic after a collision. We started to panic, as she had been asked to get to the hospital within a two-hour time frame and this didn't look as though it was going to happen now. So, we called the 101 non-urgent police number and asked for their advice.

As we did so the traffic started to slowly move, but we were asked to make our way to the hard shoulder and wait. The police at the scene of the accident could see our little blue mini, and were on their way.

Within a minute the police car pulled in front of us on the hard shoulder, and the officer came over and asked Liana to get into his car and said that he would take her to the hospital and I should then follow on as I could. It was electric watching them speed off down the hard shoulder, lights and sirens blaring, like something out of a movie!

I would have followed closely, but he drove at some speed and they were out of my vision in seconds. It took me a few minutes longer to get to the hospital and park, and when I arrived, the officer (now our friend Mike) was sitting with Liana in the corridor as she waited for her bed to become available. I was so grateful, and they were chatting away like old friends. It seemed her dream of becoming an officer herself was over, but she had just been promised a day out with Mike in his role as a traffic officer, so she was over the moon.

In fact, she had several days out over the next few months with Mike and his colleagues, and they did all they could to make Liana a part of their team when she was with them. She was even given a police hat, which I keep safely, and she made some great memories!

Liana went straight onto dialysis and the tests started for this potential kidney. She called lots of family and friends and excitedly told them the news of this potential opportunity. We knew that the person who was first on the list was at another hospital in Bristol, which we worked out meant that it was a child. Whilst we couldn't know for confidentiality reasons, of course, we knew that if it had been an adult, he or she would have been here in the same renal unit.

It was a long afternoon and evening, and Liana was cleared to go if the opportunity were to come to her and we waited in her own little cubicle. We got chatting to other patients and nurses came in regularly and reassured Liana that they still had no news. It was about 11.30pm when the doctors finally came into the room. As they approached Liana, she just gently said, 'It's okay, I know it's not my turn this time and I am praying that the other person is made well again'.

She was so incredibly brave to be like that: I had some tears, but she just accepted it in front of the doctors and we got up and left, thanking them for this opportunity anyway. She cried a few tears in the car on the way home, but we decided to call it her test run and were glad that we now knew the drill and could be better prepared for the time when it came to her for real.

It was still a blow; I can't say that it wasn't, but we were genuinely delighted for the family of the child whose life would have been changed by that gift.

The next few months were up and down: still a lot of pain and visits to hospitals, but Liana spent lots of time with friends and moved into a rented room on the same road we lived on. It was her way of taking back a little independence, while knowing she could walk across the road in the night if she was sick or scared. It worked well for her and, if I'm honest, me too – I could glance across and see her bedroom light go off at night and I knew she was okay.

We watched excitedly as other renal friends received their gift of life. We knew that it had to be growing closer for her. Each session of dialysis meant one fewer until the gift of a healthy kidney came to her.

There were multiple trips into hospital, still. Mainly because Liana refused to stick by the rules as far as eating was concerned, and she would get a bowel obstruction and be in total agony for a few days. Then I would get reports from friends that she had gone for pizza or over-eaten at a restaurant and had been struck down with pain. I understood she was unable (or unwilling) to take on board that she simply did not have the same freedom as her friends in what she ate.

There was also a pig-headedness about her, a tendency to stomp her feet and a desire to rebel a little – I get that! Although we all felt frustration that those painful hospital admissions continued time and again.

She was finally discharged from the care of the pancreas team in London. They knew that they had done all that they could, and that it was now up to Liana to be careful with her eating and make sure she was taking enough digestive enzyme.

She had started to drive herself to dialysis as she felt more in control that way, rather than waiting for a taxi to be arranged and then sometimes have to wait for up to an hour feeling grotty. This way she could just drive herself home and be in bed within minutes.

I used to look at her often and wonder how she coped with it all. I think she put on her 'brave face' so often but I could see through it, and always wondered when the next breakdown would come. They did come and quite often, mainly in private. Her struggle was emotional and revolved around her longing for a transplant that would free her from how sick she felt being on dialysis.

One particularly bad day came at the end of January 2014, after I heard her come down the street sobbing loudly. She had come home from dialysis on a Friday night and had come straight to our family home instead of her rented room. She fell into the sofa and just wailed, 'I can't do this anymore', and she cried it out and then fell asleep. At this point it had been nearly three and a half years since the start of her kidney failure and dialysis. It hurt me so much to see her in so much emotional pain: I had seen it a hundred times before and felt equally useless that I could not fix her.

I cried with her too, most times: it's just that I waited until she was out of sight. In front of her, we could conquer the world between us: I tried to make her believe this.

Sunday 26th January 2014

Liana had been visiting a friend who had recently had a kidney transplant and was having some tests. She had waited for his discharge from the hospital in Dorchester before they set off towards home later that evening. He was following her car in his own, and would soon turn off on the journey they partly shared.

I was at home, it was late in the evening and I was getting ready for work the next day and relaxing. My phone went off and a one-word text came onto my screen…'KIDNEY'.

What? Why had she sent me this?

I knew we had a deal that if I was at work with a client and couldn't answer the phone and she got her kidney transplant call, she would text me the word KIDNEY and I would down tools and come straight away; but it was a quiet Sunday evening and I was at home, so why did she text me, that is all I could think. I tried to call her, but her phone was engaged. I was scared to get excited, so I called again, remaining calm and not saying anything to anyone at home.

I still couldn't get through to her. The home phone rang, and I didn't recognise the number: I got a bad line that disconnected as quickly as I had said hello! It rang again, 'I can't hear you' I shouted! Nothing… I started to pace around like a mad woman. A few minutes later my mobile rang, and it was her, but she was crying as though something awful had happened. I panicked 'WHAT?!'

It turned out that she had been driving out of Dorchester towards home and was in a particularly bad mobile phone signal area but had seen her phone light up as it rang in the darkness and looked across to her passenger seat and saw the name of her nephrologist on the screen! She literally did an emergency stop in the middle of the road, which caused her friend to stop directly behind her. As he ran to her car wondering what the hell had happened, he found her on the phone in tears, quite inconsolable.

She knew that when her call came it would be the Transplant Co-ordinator; unless there was a potential problem with the kidney, in which case her nephrologist would call her to discuss her options. So, she knew by seeing his name on the screen what this call meant immediately...

This was her call, but she had to decide if she wanted to go ahead.

Her donor was on life-support but had passed away from a concealed cancer tumour in the brain, she was told. There was always the question about whether she should accept the kidney, and the nephrologist needed her permission to go ahead. I am extremely grateful that her friend Martin had jumped into her car and eventually had taken the phone from her, feeling that she was unable to make any sense herself. So many mixed emotions.

As I remember Liana telling me afterwards, Martin had asked the nephrologist in how many cases in a similar situation had cancer been passed from donor to recipient? The answer was none. Martin spoke on Liana's behalf and said, 'She will accept'.

He then parked up his own car at the side of the road, and drove her home in her own car to meet me and pick me up. By this time, I had decided I needed to wash my hair (very random thought) and ensure that I was ready with everything I needed. Liana's then boyfriend turned up, and Jay and Caitlin took in the news.

Liana fell through the door in floods of tears, totally unable to comprehend what had just happened. Trying not to hope too much that her nightmare of three and a half years of dialysis might be about to be behind her. That she couldn't take any more dialysis and that her dream of life without it was about to come true!

We calmed her down and she spoke to the hospital staff, who said that she could come in with one other person. Martin offered to drive her and me up there, and within minutes we were in the car en-route to Southmead Hospital, 50 miles away.

She had said goodbye to everyone at home and started to calm down and get a little excited. We knew it was going to be a long night: perhaps we underestimated just how long things would take, but we were ready, whatever it took.

We made calls in the car: she called her grandparents and family and close friends. This was her chance, she was the first on the list and her donor was pretty much a perfect match. She laughed, she cried, the emotions were all over the place.

As we arrived at the hospital, she was taken straight down to the dialysis centre and placed on the dialysis machine, potentially for the last time. This was overwhelming for her and she cried some more. We took a picture of her sticking one finger up to the machine as if to say, 'Enough, we are done!'… Eventually in the early hours we were moved up to the ward to a bed. It was about 3am and everyone else was asleep in the four-bed room so we were very quiet. Liana met her doctors, and her first question was about her donor and her family.

Of course, for privacy reasons we weren't allowed to know much, other than that her beautiful donor was a woman in her thirties from the London area who had sadly died of brain cancer. Liana cried again, and she asked about the donor family, and whether they were being cared for. Of course, no information like that would have been passed across. She genuinely wanted to make sure that they would be looked after, and how could she tell them what their gift was giving her?

She was quiet for a while as she considered their plight, their loss, their pain. Her surgeon had to tell her that it was not Liana's concern and that her focus was to be ready for this operation and for the rest of her life. She didn't like this apparent brutality, but she knew it was true; though she said straightaway that she would find them one day and tell them just how much love she had for them and their loved one.

It made her feel more than a little guilt in that her life was being potentially saved by another person's death, but she knew that this would always be the case, and she tried to accept this. She was also aware of how extremely lucky she was to have this match and, as the sun rose on the Monday morning and the surgeons did their rounds, we were told that we were waiting for Hepatitis C test results to come back clear from London to go ahead.

It was an anxious wait; we knew of course, that it could all stop in the blink of an eye. Going back home, no transplant: we knew this could happen, but we still prayed. As the morning went on we tried to sleep, both tucked in together on her bed, having been up all night; but there were many disturbances and we both had too much going on mentally to sleep. It seemed that every hour the transplant co-ordinator would come in 'No results yet, it will be soon' and then would go off again. It was torture!

It wasn't until 4pm the next day that a doctor came in and said, 'Oh yes, did you not know? Hep C is clear, so we can go ahead!' What? Oh my God! This was now real and again she cried, but this time it was with total relief.

Liana was asked to go and shower in a sterile gel to ensure that she was totally clean for surgery, and the preparation started. We knew that the kidney was on its way from London and was expected to arrive at approximately 8pm. Everything started moving fast; there was an endless stream of nurses and doctors, tests, documents to sign, information to be given, and much excitement on the renal ward. People who had known Liana at her sickest, were now so excited for her potential future. Jay and Caitlin arrived at the hospital, as did a couple of her transplant friends who lived nearby in Bristol and who wanted to wish her good luck.

I needed to get clean clothes and a few bits, so Jay and I went to a nearby supermarket whilst Liana had people with her. I walked around grabbing a few things and I felt as if I had this massive sign on my head saying, 'My baby is about to have a kidney transplant.' I wanted to tell the world, everyone, anyone who would listen! We hurried back and knew now that it was just a waiting game.

Later that evening at about 8.30pm I went out to stretch my legs, and as I passed the reception area of the ward I realised that there it was: the white human tissue bag as you see on the TV. It was being brought in by a middle-aged man who had just walked onto the ward in his ambulance clothing. I was totally overwhelmed, and gently went up to him and told him that I wanted to thank him, that this was for my darling daughter and that he had just brought with him the rest of her life. He was considerate and generous with his kind words, wished us luck and went on his way: that was it!

We had been warned that if the kidney hadn't arrived early enough we might have to wait until the next morning for the operation, as they needed to be fully staffed to deal with any occurrences post-transplant: but at 11pm they walked in and said that it was time to go, and that it was happening right now.

We walked with Liana up to the operating theatre doors: she was being wheeled on her bed, and she looked so little but so happy for the first time in years. She gave us one last wave as she was wheeled around the corner, and off she went. Jay, Caitlin & I were given access to a family room with pull-down beds and we tried to get some rest there.

Sleep came upon Jay and Caitlin, but my mind was whirring, and totally unable to shut off. It hit 1am and I went up to the ward probably about every 30 minutes to see if there was any news. It took until 3.30am for them to say that she was out of theatre and in recovery and that I could go to her. I didn't even go back downstairs to get Jay and Caitlin: I ran up the stairs and headed straight to the recovery room. There was of course, at that time of night, only one bay occupied, and the nurses smiled at me as I came into the ward. The curtains were closed, as they wanted her to rest; and as I came through the curtains she just looked up at me and quietly said, 'Yay!', lifting her thumb up.

Her donor kidney had started working and creating urine before they had even closed her up. She was catheterised (which was nothing new to her, post-op) and there was a colour to her that I hadn't seen in a few years. She smiled so much, a very sleepy smile. There was blood on her gown, more than I had expected, but it was irrelevant: she just looked incredibly well. She saidthat she finally felt free of her persistent grogginess for the first time since she got sick in 2010. After nearly four years of feeling sick, it had all lifted in an instant.

I went out down the stairs to fetch Jay and Caitlin, but stopped for a moment to ring my Dad. It was 4am and he was waiting by his phone. I sat on the stairs in the dark and just cried at him, as though I were a vulnerable child crying to a parent. I totally broke down. I had a sense of relief and fear, all in one.

Jay and Caitlin came back up with me and we spent a little while with Liana and then we all decided it was best if we left her to rest, as her blood pressure was rising a little and she needed to recover from such a serious operation. We left her, promising to return after a few hours' rest. We were totally shattered: I had now been awake for two nights and felt a wreck!

We drove away from the hospital, and as we headed out of Bristol we found a drive-through to get some food, as we were ravenous. We sat in the car park, eating; and suddenly, I totally broke down in tears, with inconsolable heavy sobbing...

We had spent years waiting for this very moment, this exact feeling: and yet somehow it was all too much. Everyone prays for salvation from misery, but I realised that you can never prepare yourself for what comes next. What does come next? The new set of fears that take over. What if it doesn't work? What if she gets sick from the immunosuppressants? What if she gets an infection and dies? What if she rejects the kidney and ends up back at square one? It all came tumbling down on me like a ton of bricks.

I realised in that moment that this was not a cure, this was just another treatment and not one that would last forever. A treatment that came with a whole new set of risks and complications. I hadn't considered this before. I really hadn't thought past this moment.

We got back home at about 6.30am and I got a few hours' sleep. Phone calls of reassurance for our family were made. A friend arrived and asked me if there was anything she could do to help, and I said, 'Yes, if you could please drive me to the hospital, as I am too tired to drive and will crash, but I need to go back.' So, she did, and we went back for about 2pm.

Liana was dozing. The lady in the bed opposite (whom we had got to know whilst waiting for this miracle) told us that Liana's nurses had closed the curtains around her bed. In her excitement, she wouldn't stop trying to get the attention of anyone passing, but she needed to rest and closing the curtains had finally made her go to sleep.

She happily drifted in and out of sleep during the afternoon. She lifted her gown and showed me the bruising that was already climbing up over her torso. Her kidney was a right sided one and had gone in very well, and was already working at 18% function and was still climbing. Their aim was to get it as high as they could, but they expected no more than 50-70%, which would be incredible! She felt amazing, she could concentrate for the first time in years, and there was the overwhelming realisation that she would now be able to read a book and take it in, and go back to her studies and do well.

They do say that you never realise just how ill you were until it stops, and this was certainly true for Liana. She was joyful at the realisation that she could begin to feel like herself again.

Six days later she was allowed home from hospital under strict infection control. No sick visitors, no trips out and she had to stay clean and healthy. Jay went and picked her up from the hospital as I was at work, and I raced home to be there before she arrived. They had to stop at a garage on the way home for Liana to use the loo (which was for staff only), but she sent Jay in to tell them that she had no choice: the kidney was working its hardest and pee she must! She scuttled into the garage in her pyjamas - as getting dressed was for people who cared what they looked like at a time like this! Nothing mattered except being well.

We settled her in at home, and then began the regular check-ups at the clinic at Southmead in Bristol. She was collected by hospital transport every other day for the first few days and then the trips became weekly, and at about this time she had the strength to drive herself up and back. A whole new range of emotions had set in. The fear about what level of function the kidney was working at became the most apparent at around this time. She became quite neurotic about it, and would panic if it so much as dropped 1%, though she was told very clearly it would be up and down for the first few weeks as it settled in.

A few weeks later we went to have her urinary stent removed which kept the link from bladder to kidney open while she healed. That was another appointment with lots of poking around but again she handled it well. Her 'bean' as she called it, was playing ball and she really felt very well.

As the weeks went on, we started to think about all the things she could do that dialysis had prevented her from doing. While she was far from 100% fit and healthy, due to constant struggles with her bowel blockages (caused by large amounts of scar tissue from the many, many operations), she was able to have a holiday and travel.

The Gift of Sunshine

We went to stay at a friend's house in Spain for a
week: Liana, Caitlin, my friend Rachel and me. The
excitement was building, and she couldn't wait
to travel again. Her final kidney function results
that week reassured her that she could go if she
continued to drink several litres of fluid each day,
which was always going to be a part of her normal
post-transplant routine. It seemed unreal as we
sat on the tarmac in the plane, and we were really
getting to take her away.

Well, as we went to take off, the plane did what
can only be described as an emergency stop
before take-off, and we all lurched forward as the
plane bounced to a halt!! Brakes smoking: the pilot
apologised for the stop due to the computer not
switching over before take-off, so we went around
the tarmac again and had a second go... No, we went
through the same scenario again, by which time
Liana proclaimed out loud, 'Oh great, I survive for all
these years and I am going to die in an aeroplane!'
I think we all chuckled, but it was a little nerve
wracking. Eventually we took off: phew!

Landing safely at Murcia airport a couple of hours
later, we walked out into the sunshine, and I think
that there were a few tears of joy at this point. Yes,
there were still complications, sickness, pain from
scar tissue and bowel problems, about 60 tablets a

day to take and rules to follow about being in the sun and what she ate, but it was total joy to be relaxing together.

We found a spot by the pool at the complex and Liana placed herself under an umbrella in the shade and felt incredible. It was a brilliant week, with swimming, food, laughter, meeting new friends and really making the most of being alive and together. We went to the beach, we walked out at night to explore, and Liana slept when she needed to, but we feasted on life. It was incredible to see both of my children laugh and be so relaxed. Of course, Liana still played the kidney card when she needed to, to get what she wanted, to send Caitlin for drinks or food, 'Pass me the sun-cream' or 'Please go and get that for me'... Of course, we all obliged, scowling at her, while having a chuckle.

The year continued with Liana having a trip to Portugal with her then boyfriend, a week of sun and fun: and then she celebrated her 22nd birthday in style with one of her best friends, Théa. They danced into the night and took a horse and carriage ride. They ate too much, and they had so much fun, and Liana was elated when she returned that she had done so much travelling in the previous weeks.

Those precious few months were interrupted at times with trips to hospital, just for a few days to deal with bowel obstruction pain and scar adhesion pain, but her 'bean' continued to thrive.

We felt that she was finally able to live her life without fear, and although her mental health had struggled so much she had an amazing group of friends, especially 'team bean' who were four girls united by the need for kidney transplants, all at different stages of their journey.

She worked hard to bring awareness to organ donation, and on many occasions attended events in town centres, shopping malls and colleges/ universities to raise awareness among the public. Being an organ donor was ferociously important to her, of course.

In her bid for more independence, Liana had moved to Bristol to live with her uncle and his family so that she could be close to a job she was given at a nail bar in Bath. It was the opportunity for her to do something that gave her a little job, though not too strenuous as she healed from a four-year battle for her health.

She was able to work just a few hours a week and had secured the job through a wonderful friend, who held a position there. They were able to look out for each other as her friend had also suffered medically for many years and understood the hospital life, dialysis included. I felt Liana was safe there and she did manage a few weeks of employment.

The Beginning of the End

Things started to deteriorate in October 2014, eight months post-transplant. Liana started to feel very unwell and likened it to how she felt when on dialysis. She started to panic and saw her consultant at clinic the next day… Tests revealed that she was rejecting her kidney transplant.

She called me, crying like a baby on the phone, and screaming at me that she couldn't do this again… I encouraged her to stay positive, and headed to the hospital to be with her. After more thorough tests, it was found that she was in acute rejection and it wasn't going to stop anytime soon. Her liver function tests were going crazy too and she was admitted back to the nephrology ward.

When I got there she just howled with pain, emotional pain: it was so frightening for her to feel this unwell again, and so unfair to have this thrown back on her when she had been doing so well. It was decided that the only way she was going to have a chance at keeping the kidney was to have an intense course of treatment in a High Dependency Unit to obliterate her immune system. Her doctor explained that it wasn't a nice treatment and that she had to be prepared for how it would make her feel. But, she was going to do anything to keep her 'bean', and so it started.

She was transferred to the HDU and the next day the ten-day course of treatment started. It was an intense few hours each day. The drug went into her intravenously via a tube in her neck and it made her whole little body seize up for hours, unable to move; she was in so much pain, but she knew it was what she needed to get the result she was begging for: she would do anything for this, as she was so committed to her gift of life and she wasn't ready to let it go.

Her whole body ached, right to the bones: she couldn't move as the drug got pushed in over the course of each day, then as it finished, within a couple of hours she could sit up again and take a few steps to the bathroom. This meant that we had to wear face masks and gowns when we were at her side, which of course, we continued to be each day. It was hot sitting there draped in plastic, but nothing compared to what she was enduring.

The treatment was a four-hour infusion but was having such a horrid effect on her little body they gave it to her over eight hours. The side-effects were hideous.

So, the immune system was destroyed, and eight days in we started to see the results we wanted and her 'bean' woke up again... Slowly, slowly, the function started to improve, and she could tell it was working. It had been such a scary few days that we were incapable of feeling any elation, just caution.

Eventually, Liana was moved to a side room. She was still neutropenic (without an immune system) so she had to be very careful who was allowed in to visit. In fact, Liana was very firm about this, and vetted anyone who wanted to come in. Her health was all she cared about.

It was now the end of October, and our aim was to get her home for Christmas. In mid-November we were permitted to go to the café downstairs for a hot drink. A couple of weeks later, we were allowed a few hours outside the hospital and Liana simple wish was to go to McDonalds! So, the four of us sat in the car at a drive-through and she thought all her Christmases had come at once. We were able to take her to the shopping mall, and even though she wore a face mask, she enjoyed her time out.

She had got past caring about people staring at her for being so clearly unwell. She had got used to it many years before, when she had had a feeding tube inserted down into her stomach via her nostril for a few months, to help with her nutrition when she was vomiting all day. We had walked through many towns and shops, and I honestly thought that I would kill the next person who gawped at her as though she was a freak on display. But, she told me she really didn't give a shit, and that people could stare. I hated it, as it made me feel so over-protective and I wanted them to stop, but people just stared. It would have been kinder for them to ask her, 'How does that help you?' or, 'How are you?' but alas... I guess it is human nature to stare at something which is outside our normal experience.

At the beginning of December, she was able to come home, and things looked as though they were heading in the right direction. She was on a different course of immunosuppressants and her kidney was doing what it needed to do. She still had a lot of sickness and an upset tummy, but we could manage that at home.

Within a week Liana was on her way up to London for a night out with friends! Most of us would have taken things more slowly but she wasn't like that… ever! She had also been in touch with a journalist from *The Sunday Times* newspaper. He had contacted her about an article he was writing on organ donation, especially concerning high-risk transplants. Liana had been in the media spotlight so many times over the previous few years that she took it in her stride to do an interview with him in North London, not far from her old hospital.

They met, and this is the interview the editor sent me

The recent news that a quarter of all deceased organs used in transplants are considered 'marginal' - taken from the elderly, cancer sufferers and drug abusers - can be put into some sort of perspective by the story of Liana Tolland. I meet the bubbly, 22-year-old from Yeovil in a café just off Shaftesbury Avenue while she's doing some Christmas shopping. She admits to being tired then puts it down to a late night, clubbing.

She apologises because her face is a little puffy from the steroids she has to take. A year ago the idea of travelling up to London would have been ludicrous, let alone dancing till 4am. Her entire life revolved around dialysis treatment three times a week. She was as weak as a kitten and falling apart mentally. "My last session, I couldn't take it anymore," she says, with a shake of the head. "You feel all right at the beginning because it's cleaning you, but by the end you feel like you're dying. I was at a real low ebb so I asked to come off. I just sat there in tears. My nurse said, 'It could be tomorrow!' but she'd been saying 'it could be tomorrow' for ages."

The 23rd of this month marks 60 years since the first ever successful kidney transplant. Up until former US army plastic surgeon Joseph Murray's success with a pair of twins in Boston, 1954, the operation was considered impossible. Murray later received the Nobel Prize in Medicine. Since his breakthrough that Christmas in 1954 more one million people worldwide have had their lives saved by the gift of a kidney, 69,000 of them in the UK. However demand means that there are currently over 5,800 people waiting for one here.

It took three-and-a-half years to find Liana a match but that doesn't take into account the 18 months of illness during which she was considered too poorly to receive one. Her ordeal began in 2010 with an allergic reaction to malaria tablets she was taking while volunteering in Uganda. Her pancreas split open and massive internal bleeding caused all her organs to shut down. She nearly died, came back from the brink, then nearly died again when another reaction to medication caused brain seizures and knocked out her kidneys for good. When she finally left hospital, she faced a life of dialysis until a donor could be found. "I went from not having a care to fighting for my life every day," she says. "I was an emotional wreck and my family were going through it, too. You have to think you're not going to get one because you need to live day-to-day."

*Another Christmas in hospital went by. Then on
January 26 at 8.30pm in the evening, her mobile
rang. "I saw it was the hospital's number and there
was no reason to call unless it was a kidney," she
recalls. "I was shaking when I put the phone down."
There was a catch. The donor kidney was 'high risk',
a woman who had died from a cancerous brain
tumour. There was a possibility of hepatitis B, too
(early tests were for hepatitis C). Liana spent the
next day in hospital chewing her nails while they
ran checks. "I knew her heart was still beating inside
her in a room somewhere nearby, but that her life
ending meant that mine might begin again," she
says, staring into her cup. The hospital decided to
go ahead with the operation. The new kidney began
working immediately, flushing out her system. "Even
though I was groggy I could feel it kick in," she says.
"It was like a switch had been thrown. Before it was
like I had a permanent fog in my mind. I couldn't even
concentrate on reading. The moment I had the new
kidney the fog was gone. The next day I was able to
read properly. I could absorb the words."*

*The likelihood that her kidney will not last, might
even present complications further down the line,
doesn't bother Liana. "I know I'll need another kidney
one day but I'm so glad I have this one," she says. "It
could last another day or decades. But if it gave up
tomorrow I'd be grateful for the 11 months it's given
me. I can't be dreading it packing up or I won't be
able to live my life with any normality."*

*Liana's was one of 3,054 kidney transplants in
Britain last year. Of those, 1,940 came from deceased*

donors and another 1,114 came from living people
- 118 of them from altruistic donors, non-family
members who give one in an act of selfless generosity.
The organisation, Give A Kidney, helps publicise the
cause, with donations on the rise. On average a kidney
from a deceased donor will last for a decade, that rises
to 12 years for one from a living donor.

However, demand for organs is increasing and
that has meant more marginal ones being accepted.
Inevitably there are failures, like the case of Darren
Hughes and Robert 'Jim' Stuart, two men from Wales
whose donor kidneys turned out to be infected with
a deadly parasitic worm. Theirs is an extreme case,
maintains Ben Lindsey, consultant vascular and renal
transplant surgeon at London's Royal Free Hospital:
"We tread a fine line because we don't want to
waste organs. With deceased organs, decisions are
sometimes made late at night when there is less
information than would be preferable. They are
subjective judgements based on age, medical history
and potential high-risk behaviour but they are taken
very carefully." On the flipside, NHS figures show that
the five-year survival rate for transplant patients is
more than double the 35.8% survival rate for dialysis
patients.

"I'm sure my kidney was rejected by another
hospital," shrugs Liana. "But it's not like they are
deliberately going to make you worse. People don't
realise the risk of dialysis. I've had people die right
in front of me. When you see that you can't be scared
of receiving a kidney. I'd take one with a risk of dying
every time."

*The road since her transplant has its setbacks
- there was another allergic reaction to the
immunosuppressant drugs she has to take daily - but
now Liana's world has stabilised. She has a boyfriend,
who comes along to our meeting. She is planning to
re-embark on a career working with young offenders.
Most importantly, she feels she finally has a future. "It's
like someone telling you you're going on the most
amazing holiday of your life, but you don't know when.
Pack a bag and get ready," she says, blinking hard. "It
could be any time between now and never."*

...

Two days after this meeting Liana was sick again
and back in hospital. The risks of dehydration and
complications are high with a kidney transplant, so
she knew she had to go back in. Still as determined
as ever to make it home in time for Christmas, she
did everything in her power to get better. Except,
this time we got some rather different news; the
sickness wasn't the normal bowel obstruction: it was
CMV(Cytomegalovirus), a herpes style infection that
80% of us carry without symptoms, but Liana had
been clear a few weeks earlier, and it was felt that
she had caught this bug in hospital whilst she had
had zero immune system.

She was given a course of antibiotics and allowed
home a few days later, on Christmas Eve afternoon
in fact. Talk about close to the wire.

Christmas was as normal, for the first time in years. We had recently moved home, and the girls did their usual routine of early bedtime together in new pyjamas, something that they had done for years, since childhood. This ritual gave them so much excitement and it was lovely to re-live this old habit. My lovely Dad joined us for Christmas Day lunch and we played board games and ate too much. Liana took time out to relax when she needed a break, but otherwise it was a fabulous day of family and festive food.

On Boxing Day, Jay and I had booked flights to see friends in Pennsylvania, USA; we had been hesitant to go, but Liana reassured us she was well enough, and Caitlin would be with her. Also, her boyfriend would join them and stay for the few days we would be away. I think they had as much fun as we did being away, having the house to themselves and eating too much. We spoke daily, and we used FaceTime when we could to check that things were okay, and they were.

We came home on 2nd January after the NYE celebrations, and the truth about Liana having needed a trip to hospital came forward. They had asked a friend to take her to A&E and felt that it wasn't necessary to tell us. It was a quick twenty-four hours in the ward whilst the pain died down, and it was a routine she had done dozens of times over the years and she was well known at the local hospital, so they had had it under control in no time.

January 6th turned out to be the last time that Liana would be admitted to hospital. Her stomach and bowel issues continued, and it appeared that this infection wasn't happy, so her transplant hospital asked her to come in... Just to be safe... Blood tests were done, and twenty-four hours later she was given the news that the infection was much worse, which explained her dreadful tummy pain and upset. A new course of tablets was arranged, and we started to get a little more concerned that this wasn't going away. We continued to visit each day, or night according to work schedules, and found her looking pretty exhausted and fed up.

On Sunday 18th January 2015, I arrived with a close friend to visit Liana, and she wasn't any better. We took her for a sneaky hot chocolate down at the café in the hospital, and when we came back to the ward I noticed for the first time that she became out of breath just climbing up onto the bed. She realised that she was breathless, too. I think if I am honest, this was the day I realised that we wouldn't win, this time. Having Googled throughout every second of her illness, I had already noted that CMV in the lungs (CMV Pneumonitis) was fatal in immunocompromised patients, which of course she was. Panic quietly crept into me and I kept it to myself.

Leaving her there that night was tough, and I arrived early the next day. I was in time to see the consultant who had told her that the drugs clearly weren't stopping the virus and it was necessary to consider other options. There was an unlicensed drug in Europe (not licensed in the UK) that they could get by special measures with the health board, and that she would have to sign for informed patient consent. She said that of course she would sign, but she became scared that this drug would mean losing her kidney. When she expressed this concern to the consultant, his reply was stark: 'Liana, this is about more than your kidney, this is about keeping you alive now'. Then he left the room.

She sat very calmly, and I, on the other hand, started to cry. 'Why are you crying?' she asked... 'I can't live without you, Liana' I told her... She replied very sternly, 'Yes Mum, you can, and you have no choice because you have to look after my sister'... She meant nothing more than that. She made me assure her that I would always be there for Caitlin, and she seemed to indicate that she could live with the rest. She adored her sister, I already knew that, but this was in deadly earnest.

The week saw her deterioration take place quite rapidly. On the Wednesday, four days after she first became breathless, her lungs were clearly giving up. Caitlin had come to join me on a visit, as she lived close by at Uni, and it was clear to us both then that Liana was starting to panic at the lack of breath. She was beginning to have panic attacks: and she had one quite brutal one in front of us. A nurse saw Liana trying to climb to a window to get any air she could. She really couldn't breathe; yet she was on strong oxygen.

The new medication was being given through an IV line, but it didn't seem to bring the results we had urgently hoped for. In fact, it was doing nothing and her infection markers were out of control. By the Thursday she had been moved to the High Dependency Unit because she was unable to breathe. Eventually and she accepted a blood transfusion (which went against a future kidney transplant), but she was compelled by the realisation that she was running out of options. It gave her a little help as the new blood oxygenated her system, but she was scared now and her body was totally exhausted. She struggled to climb out of bed, with help, to use the commode next to her bed. It was painful to watch, and she wasn't winning this battle.

She had no fear of being on life-support, having come through it on three other occasions during the past few years, and she was begging them to let her sleep. Overnight on the Thursday, I walked behind her bed as they wheeled her to the ICU, and again she begged them to let her sleep so that she could stop struggling. Her breathing was shallow and painful, gasping really. She drifted for most of the night, but when she jolted back to consciousness she was scared.

Friday morning doctors' rounds saw the head of the ICU appear, and she again said to him, 'Let me sleep': and this time it was agreed that the safer option was to allow her to rest, and life-support was decided upon. She was relieved, as she knew this routine and they worked quickly to stop her pain; the anaesthetist came within minutes, and they prepared her. The milky liquid in the syringe went slowly in and I held her hand. I suddenly panicked that this might be my last chance with her awake, so I said quickly, "I love you, I love you, I love you' and she just whispered to me, 'I love you Mum' and off to sleep she went.

Saying Goodbye

Arrangements were made for me to sleep at the ICU unit and I quickly became accustomed to the routine of sitting with her by day, taking the odd break when family arrived to go and shower or sit in the chapel and pray. I never woke feeling able to eat, and it took until about 5pm each day before my body nudged me into leaving Liana's side to find some nutrition. I went back to my little room with a single bed and a fridge and a shared shower at about 11pm at night, and was back in her little room by 7am each day.

After a few days, the team removed her muscle relaxant, so that they could see how she would respond; she was still sedated but I am sure she knew I was there. Each time I put my face to hers and whispered in her ear, she would gently move her head a little or shrug her shoulders. I thought that I was dreaming it, but it was witnessed by so many and it gave me hope that she knew that I was near. We talked to her all the time, and I bathed her with the nurses, but she wasn't doing well.

It was decided to nurse her in a prone position; when lying on your front, the lungs have more room to expand. This helped for a day or so and then she was returned to her back, but she started to deteriorate again.

Both Jay and Caitlin had dreadful colds and coughs and were asked not to come near Liana for fear of infection, so my Mum came to be with me each day by 8am, and other friends and family arrived to see Liana and support us all. The care that we received was incredible, yet I felt so alone; even sitting in a room with a dozen people, I just felt alone.

Sleep eluded me, with my mind racing; I knew we were heading towards the end, but I was scared to say it out loud. I went down to the A&E department one night and asked to see a doctor to get myself some sleeping tablets on the advice of the ICU doctor. They helped me to sleep deeply, but they didn't take away any of my pain.

The support we received never faltered. Friends kept in touch, in person, by text and phone call and even through social media. One night an online candle vigil was started, and it went viral, and friends of friends all over the world were lighting candles and praying for Liana's recovery. I asked a million questions each day of anyone who would listen, anyone who might give me any hope at all that they could bring her back.

Two weeks passed, and we seemed to go up and then down again, and more times than seemed fair; one better blood test (they were hourly), and then the next one would be back to bad. On the Thursday morning, I took a photo of the DLC tattoo on Liana's wrist: before leaving for Uganda, she had our initials (Diana, Liana, Caitlin) inscribed in italics so that she could take us with her everywhere. I took my photo over to the tattoo shop opposite the hospital, and they placed the ink in the same place on my own wrist. It meant so much to me that I had this now and I wanted to show her: I hoped I could one day.

On Friday, things were going downhill. I hadn't seen Jay or Caitlin for a few days as they had been so poorly, but I was told they could come in, so I rang them. They protested, 'We are still sick' but I told them what the doctors had told me. 'It's not a cold that will take her, it won't make any difference now, you need to come'. They got angry with me for saying this! How could I say such a thing? But I was only repeating what I knew; I wasn't trying to be hurtful or to exaggerate: it was this bad for real.

An application had been made to the Royal Brompton Hospital in London for Liana to be transferred there for ECMO (Extracorporeal membrane oxygenation is an extracorporeal technique of providing prolonged cardiac and respiratory support to persons whose heart and lungs are unable to provide an adequate amount of gas exchange or perfusion to sustain life.) The response had not come through when we went to bed that night, the three of us sleeping in a little side room. I didn't sleep, the others did: but they were sick, I knew what was coming, and even if they didn't want to believe it, I knew.

I had the feeling that Liana had already left her body earlier that afternoon. I sat with Liana, holding her hand, talking to her and telling her that it was okay to leave. Then I went to the outside door to let Jay and Caitlin in as they had just called my mobile phone, so that I'd click the door buzzer. When I got back to her bedside I just said to her, 'Look, we are all here now', and I picked up her hand again and it felt different. Her hand looked empty, like a little birds' nest of a hand, with nothing there under her skin: she had changed, and I felt it. I didn't want to believe it, but I felt it.

I was so aware that others were still thinking in their minds, she could do this. She had pulled through so many, many times before when she shouldn't have, so I really felt that I wanted to spend some time alone with Liana. I got out of my bed at about 6am and wandered in through to her side. Still nothing from the hospital in London, as we had been assured that they would wake us to go with her if the call came in the night.

A familiar face stood writing notes at her bedside, a nephrologist we had met a few times before; in fact the one that had told us that the kidney transplant was going ahead, just a year previously. I asked him about the transfer to London and he gently told me that they had declined to take her, explaining that they felt that they could get her on to the lung bypass machine but that they would fail to get her off it again, so they weren't willing to take her. That was enough, no more: I told him that I wanted this to stop, and he said he felt he agreed; but he wanted to ring Liana's nephrologist and run through things with him first, and that the ICU team had to have a final chat.

Letting Go

'It's okay to go,' I told her even though I knew she wasn't able to hear me. 'I promise you I will be okay, I promise'…

I took the time just to be alone with her until the ICU team came to sit with me. 'Please let her go,' I asked them, and they agreed that it was the right thing to do. I told the wonderful doctor that I had to go and wake my husband and daughter up, and that I needed his support with them as they wouldn't accept this decision as I had, through their own pain; and he agreed that we would have a family meeting and that he would take them through why it had to happen, and that another twenty-four hours sadly wasn't an option now.

It was time to stop the fight: she had been through too much now and I really felt that I didn't want her to go through any more. They explained gently that even if she were to survive, she would have a tracheostomy (the creation of a temporary or permanent opening into the trachea to aid breathing) for the rest of her life and would lose any chance of a further transplant: and therefore dialysis would be her only option, and she would not live for much longer as the infection was rife.

They say that at critical times like this everything slows down, as though you're wading through treacle, and they are right. We fell into the next process; we were treated with such respect and given time. We sat with Liana and we all cried. It was hard to believe that we had reached this point. It didn't make sense.

Our good friends Nicky and Iain turned up to be with us, as they had come to Bristol to support us while we waited for news of her transfer to London. When they realised what had happened overnight they asked us what we wanted; I asked them to stay with us.

I called a few people, quietly, outside the room in the corridor, and told them what was happening next. I asked my Mum and her husband to go and be with my Dad, who lived alone and was himself aged and ill of health. I was so anxious about how he would react, and I didn't want him to be alone. I rang Liana's aunt in Ireland, and her Grandad in America; we all wept together, and I assured them that I would stay by her side all the time. I spoke to my sister: I wanted to go back to being a child again with her, to a time when we were unaware of such pain, but I had to fight this head on. It was my last role as Liana's mum: it was the last thing I could do for her.

It was about 11.30am and we were all by her bedside and nothing was happening. Not that I knew what to expect, so I asked the nurse in charge of Liana on that shift when they would turn off her life-support. He replied that it would be when we were ready and not before, and that they would support her until such time as we felt ready. I realised now that everything for them was about supporting us through our journey, as they knew that nothing more could be done for Liana.

'Please do it now, go ahead,' I told him, and he went to speak to the doctors. The other option was that I never said to do it; and we would sit here for hours or days crying at her bedside, which would have hurt only us, not her; but it would have been delaying the inevitable and there was never going to be a right time: it was never going to be okay.

We asked what would happen, and they gently explained that they would keep her asleep with sedation but that they would turn off the adrenaline which was supporting her heart and keeping it beating. We were told that it wouldn't probably be an instant thing, that her body would fight to keep working for a while, and it did. The drugs were stopped at 11.45am and we sat with her, stroked her face, held her, said all we needed to say to her. I told her I would be okay; I knew she would worry about leaving me, but I needed to give her permission to go.

I asked for the hospital Chaplain to come and help us to say prayers for Liana. She came quickly and we all held hands around Liana's bed; I held Liana's hand on one side, with the Chaplain at the other side. We all listened as she thanked Liana for her love and for the time that she was on this Earth. It was a moment of comfort but still it was painful. It seemed so unreal that we had to be doing this at all. Her blessings helped, and I was grateful.

Liana's skin was dewy soft, and although she was pale in comparison to her normal rosy cheeks, she was beautiful, just peaceful and beautiful: I thought I might die with her, and my heart was literally aching for her.

I asked the ICU consultant if she could be an organ donor herself but he explained that she couldn't, as the infection had ravaged her organs which could not be safely transferred. I was relieved, though I felt awful for feeling relieved; as much as I knew that it would have been what she would have wanted, I couldn't bear the thought of them touching her any more. The years of endless operations and dialysis, feeding tubes, wounds, pain and infection were enough; I just wanted them to leave her alone. I felt ashamed that I wanted to keep her intact when there had been this courage shown by her own donor's family just a year previously, but I couldn't bear any more pain. I just wanted her to be left alone, and that is the only way I can explain it.

We asked lots of questions: what would happen? How would we know? The monitors were silenced but we kept looking at them, waiting for her pressure to go below the number 15, as apparently that would mean that she had given up the fight. Her numbers dropped for a while but then stabilised. I was sitting on one side of her and Caitlin on the other. Jay was behind me and our friends were at the bottom of the bed. My friend Nicky had been my birthing partner with Liana as I was a single parent, and it was surreal that she too would be with me at her death. We were in it together again.

I held my hand on Liana's left arm, at the point of her dialysis fistula which gave her the strongest pulse. I felt her heart beating and beating, scared that each time would be the last beat.

When the phone rang in the ICU room, the nurse asked me if we would allow two of Liana's renal nurses who had cared for her so much to come down and say goodbye. The news had filtered through and they were devastated. Of course, it would be an honour for them to see her. A few minutes later they arrived, anxiously, and stood at the bottom of her bed, tears in their eyes. I stood up for the first time in two hours and went to hug one of them, crying. As I did so, I heard Caitlin cry out, 'She's gone!'... I turned to the monitor and it was blank: I screamed at everyone to get out, and to leave me alone with her and for us to be alone as a family for one last time; but I didn't mean it, I just didn't know what to do or say.

I grabbed her, pulling her up from the bed from her waist into my arms, and laid my head on her tummy and felt the warmth of her skin – I could hear a loud noise in the room, like a wailing sound: it was so loud, but I realised that it was me, this noise coming from my body that I hadn't heard before. The sound scared me: it was the sound of pain, the pain of a mother losing her child, this mother losing this child.

It was chaos in the room for a while, yet it was peaceful at the same time. I noticed so many things; I held Caitlin and felt her shaking, too. I hurt for her, I hurt for me. I knew we had just done the right thing, but my mind was still spiralling; it was unreal, a dream, a nightmare, I don't know: I couldn't identify with this amount of pain. One minute of screaming, the next just holding her, my little girl, that was it: it was all over.

We left the room for a while, about an hour later, to give the medical team time to remove her tubes and breathing apparatus, and to make her look more presentable. I had already pulled down out of a bun her lashings of long chestnut brown hair, and it framed her face beautifully. When we were outside the room I was able to make a few calls to my Mum and to Liana's paternal Grandad in America – I am unsure if I even spoke, my silence speaking the words that none of them wanted to hear. I think I just said, '2.06pm', and I kept saying sorry, as if I wanted to not be saying this and dragging them into the grief, too.

I remember holding Caitlin out in the corridor and telling her in no uncertain terms that while she was about to watch her mother fall apart, that I would be okay: I promised her that I would be able to deal with this and that I would always be there for her, too. I felt her fear, and it seemed amazing to me that I was capable of focusing on her and providing the reassurance she needed. It gave me hope, too.

We went back in to be with Liana and we all spent a little time with her; we had access to a family room, and of course I had the room I had been sleeping in for the last two weeks just next door. Other family members arrived and we all waded through the treacle together. Liana's step-dad arrived with some of his family; he had brought Liana up in her younger, formative years and it was agonising to see his pain too. My mother arrived with her husband; a few close friends arrived and some other family who had been coming to see Liana that day anyway: and

I said that they could still come if they wanted to pay their respects, which of course they did.

I didn't spend much time with Liana that afternoon: everyone else went in and out, and the emotion was just so incredibly tough. We all huddled together in support of each other. Old arguments were laid to rest, and nothing mattered any more, only that we needed to work our way together through this pain.

It was about 7pm when we all felt that it was time to leave. I started to panic at leaving her there, and I wanted to be the last person to kiss her goodbye. I wanted to be on my own with her, so everyone else went and said their final goodbyes and then I went in on my own.

I remember feeling a little scared; I hadn't been with a dead person before in my life, and while so many others had told me it would be peaceful, and they would look beautiful and at peace, I didn't find it that way. I was shocked at how cold she was when I kissed her, and whilst I would love her forever I didn't want to be in that room there with her. I told her, 'I love you baby, but I have to go', and I picked up her bag and looked round one last time. It didn't feel like it was her, just her shell: I knew she wasn't there, and I felt little connection with her except raw grief. I got outside the door and crashed down to the floor; my legs just went from under me. Family came and got me, and I was taken to my room with everyone close by.

I couldn't leave her there: so I asked them to take her away first, to the mortuary, away from the ICU, so that I felt that she was leaving me and not that I was leaving her. Family made sure that I knew what was going on, and I was told when the porters had arrived and how they took her away gently on the bed, covered. Her step-father (my first husband) had walked down the corridor to the lift with her. He thanked the porters and came back to us as a group.

I cannot explain why hearing of this final parting helped me. The last fatherly act had been completed. I was grateful, and it soothed a little of my pain: it was such a loving and generous thing to do. Leaving the hospital, we all walked together.

Staff had been thanked, and it was now about 8pm and dark and cold outside. It was 7th February 2015. Always, now, the day she left.

We all got to our cars, and I don't know how my legs carried me: I was screaming and crying out and being held as we got to the car. It was totally surreal, and it dawned on me that after four and a half years there would be no more hospitals; yet that was all we had known, it was a part of our lives and it too was leaving us. There was a feeling in me of, 'Oh, I actually don't have to have this fear anymore' but the only reason I no longer feared she would die was real for all the wrong reasons.

We travelled away in different cars going different directions. Jay drove me, and Nicky sat in the back of the car with me. Caitlin went with her half-sister and they drove my car back to Yeovil, and other family all left together. It was an awful feeling, and I don't remember much about that night: I climbed up the front steps of my house, devoid of all feeling, totally numb, and with no idea how to function without her.

Remembering

What happened in the next few days was just about clinging together, helping each other. Friends arrived, they stayed to support us, Nicky and Iain slept at our home for a few nights and family arrived each day. We seemed to be stronger in numbers and took a huge amount of comfort from those around us. We cried together but we also laughed together. We shared memories and they helped me to go through things that needed to be done.

On the Monday morning our GP from the local surgery called me. He had received notification from the hospital about Liana's passing and was so devastated that he rang me. He knew us so well and his voice broke. He apologised for crying, and I comforted him. I told him what I had learned, that 'because of people like him, people like me, got to spend more time with people like her' and that was what he needed to remember if ever there was a time when being a GP got too tough. I really believe in that moment he understood me, and I have said those words to so many other health professionals that we met on our journey; without them, none of this would have happened and we would have lost her years before. I wanted them to stand proud.

We had been given a phone number to call at the hospital on the Monday morning to make an appointment to go back and register her death. We were also advised to find a funeral director who would arrange to collect her body. It seemed ridiculous to be doing this for her, just unreal.

Back at the hospital on the Wednesday, we waited nervously to sign the documents to release her body to the funeral director. Then we sat with the registrar and she gently took us through all that needed to be done.

I remembered registering Liana's birth twenty-two years before: how could I now be registering her death? I was handed the certificate and asked to sign it as her next of kin. I cried, as I didn't realise I would have to sign it: it was as though I was accepting her death had happened, and I didn't want to, as if I was signing it to say it was okay she had died. I cried so much, and the registrar was totally understanding; both she and Jay supported me, and we got through the appointment, somehow.

Afterwards, we decided to go up to the renal ward and say thank you to all the team who had looked after Liana for all those years. There was a different air on the ward, and it seemed quieter; when staff saw us they were so full of emotion and so upset that it was humbling to see just how much they had cared for her, how much this affected them, too. We spoke with her esteemed team, and we made sure that they were aware of just how grateful we were; their care was outstanding, and they always went that extra mile: even if it was sitting with her eating biscuits and drinking tea at 4am, they always gave her whatever comfort she needed.

There is no guide on how to lose a child. In fact, I remember saying, 'I lost her' and then correcting myself. If you lose something, it is because you were careless of it; and I did nothing but care for her, every day in her childhood and certainly every day during her illness: so I did not lose her.

So many rallied to help us, yet I took the lead in calling the funeral director and we made an appointment to discuss our requirements. I couldn't even say the word funeral, let alone coffin, and it twisted my guts to even think how I could deal with this day that we had ahead of us.

We chose a very simple service of remembrance for Liana at the Crematorium in Yeovil; I refused a cortege of vehicles and I feared driving behind her coffin would be too much to bear. We chose to use a humanist celebrant for the service as we are not religious, and Liana wouldn't have wanted a church service; a simple service and cremation was all I could deal with and we started to work with the humanist celebrant on what would happen during the service.

The service was at 1pm on 19th Feb 2015. We faced the day almost like robots carrying out the actions we had to do at certain times, but with an unspoken anxiety. It was cold and drizzly as we arrived at the Crematorium, and the hundreds of people who were gathered outside gave me so much warmth. I couldn't face getting out of the car to speak to anyone, so we sat there for a while: our tears were unstoppable. Eventually, the funeral director came over to us in the car and said that Liana had arrived and that the car was waiting to pull up, and asked us if we wanted to walk with her.

We all got out of the car, and Caitlin and I alone walked over to be with her. We walked in front of the funeral car carrying her to the front door. Holding onto each other as we took each painful step.

I couldn't look anyone in the eye, for fear I couldn't handle my emotions. I was overwhelmed with the sheer number of people: friends and family, staff and friends from the hospital, and others who knew Liana from school, including teachers. I watched as the undertakers started to pull her coffin from the rear of the car and onto the shoulders of the pallbearers: Jay, Frank (Liana's step-father who raised her), Iain (who had been with us as Liana passed) and Liana's boyfriend. I saw their utter agony as they tried to maintain their dignity and do what was right for Liana, her family and everyone gathered to honour her.

As we entered, they played Liana & Caitlin's favourite song, 'Sweet Disposition' by Temper Trap (lyrics below). I held Caitlin as we followed the coffin, just the two of us, as everyone else was waiting inside.

Sweet Disposition

Never too soon
Oh, reckless abandon
Like no one's watching you
A moment a love
A dream aloud
A kiss a cry
Our rights

Our wrongs
A moment, a love
A dream aloud
A moment, a love
A dream, aloud
So stay there
'Cause I'll be coming over
And while our blood's still young
It's so young, it runs
And won't stop 'til it's over
Won't stop to surrender
Songs of desperation
I played them for you
A moment, a love
A dream aloud
A kiss, a cry
Our rights
Our wrongs
A moment, a love
A dream aloud
A moment, a love
A dream aloud
Stay there
'Cause…

The service was beautiful, simple and dignified. A photo of Liana was at the side of her coffin and an overwhelming feeling of love poured out. There were too many people to fit into the space and people were in corridors and in the reception area, listening to the service.

The last act I could do at this time was to read my own words: they had been written at another wakeful 4am. I will share what I said, below...

"Even to think about her bounding through the door makes me smile. It was never a quiet affair, Liana entering a room. You would hear her before you saw her and then the whirlwind that would ensue could sometimes be devastating!

If you were talking, she'd join in; if you were eating, she'd steal your food; if you were concentrating, you could forget it; if you were resting, well, you weren't any longer; if Jay and I were sitting together, she would sit on top of us until we let her squeeze in the middle! She was quite possibly the most annoying person many of you ever met!

She was in the room and you knew it... But, with her came something unique, something many of us witnessed and it is ultimately what has drawn us all here today... She made you fall in love with her, she made you stare at her, she made you laugh with her, and feel her energy sparkling. Liana was REALLY alive.

I was never sure how anyone could win some of the battles of the last four years. When doctors said she couldn't do it, she did. When everyone else would have given up, she dug her heels in. I am aware that on many occasions she faked it to make it, she hid her pain to protect me, and that she saw the pain in my eyes as I watched it all getting too much for her. But I do believe the last four years were her gift to me. How many of us really get the time to sit with our children for such an intense time, week after week,

month after month, laughing, crying, adjusting to bad
news together, and celebrating little victories together.
We created havoc even in the hospitals, and would
be found screaming with laughter when nobody
understood how we could even be smiling. Only
Liana would use her drip stand as a skate board down
hospital corridors and cry with laughter when she hit
the wall and fell on the floor!

So, is losing your daughter hell? It may be, but not
as hellish as watching her fighting for her life for four
years. Taking on this new and different pain is another
duty as her mother, one that I will bear because I know
she no longer has any pain at all.

The last words Liana spoke were 'I love you Mum', a
beautiful gift, but the biggest gift of all was choosing
me to be your Mum at all. I love you darling girl –
didn't we have great fun?"

We sat in quiet reflection, listening to a lovely piece
called 'Dancing in the Sky'. The committal was said,
and that noise came again, the one that was so loud
on the day she died. It was that noise I made. It came
from deep down inside. It was me.

The service ended with the music 'Don't Worry,
Be Happy', as this was a song everyone associated
with Liana as after her transplant she videoed herself
singing this as she inhaled the helium from all the
balloons she was sent post-operatively! It was a
happy song but the whole place was weeping. I
stood outside as everyone filed out and paid their
respects, and I was hugged a thousand times.
Everyone was with us, we felt it deeply.

We asked only for family flowers, and for donations to be made to Live Life Give Life, and a JustGiving page was set up in Liana's memory,

https://www.justgiving.com/fundraising/lianatollandtribute

where we have now raised over £16,000 in her name through various channels. Donations made purely from love, different fundraisers, and even a cycle ride from London to Bristol and Yeovil by three of Liana's friends who wanted to cycle the route from her hospitals to her home. Work donations in offices and shops have added to the total... It is overwhelming just how much we have achieved in her name.

We gathered in a local hotel, close family and friends, to remember Liana; and we had a beautiful tree set up with tags upon which mourners could write their memories of Liana. It was amazing to see the impact she had had on so many people, who had laughed with her, and who remembered her for so much fun and naughtiness!

The day gave us all the strength in numbers to move forward together and be strong.

You should never have to bury your child. Nothing more needs to be said.

"The reality of child loss is that the wrong can never be made right. You can't fix it, mend it, or cry it away. No matter what, someone is always missing. No matter what, my family is achingly incomplete."
Angela Miller

Making Sense Of It

When I decided to write Liana's story, I wanted there to be a part of it that helps to move anyone in this situation forward, even just a little step on the massive journey that is grief, to try and make sense of the child-loss grief journey that I am now on.

Grief for anyone known and beloved, whatever the relationship, is painful; agony at times, a relief on occasions when there has been a lot of suffering; but it is mainly totally overwhelming at first.

Except when it is the grief for the loss of a child. Then it seems that the overwhelming feelings will never go away.

You hear people say, 'There is no loss like the loss of a child' and 'Nobody should ever have to bury their child', and other similar words of platitudes. They are right. It is totally unnatural for this to happen, no matter what the age of the child or parent. We all know the rule of thumb when it comes to who passes in the proper world order: the older generations pass before the next, and the next, etcetera...

I dearly hope that this is not a pain that you will ever feel; and that you are reading this story to learn a little more about the inspirational person who was my daughter, Liana. Or perhaps you would like to try to understand more clearly how you can help someone you love with their own loss.

There is one thing that all parents bereaved of their lost child agree to, and that is that we NEVER want anyone else to know what this pain is really like. We have joined a group that nobody should have to join, and we didn't choose this; we fell into it from a thousand feet up, landing heavily on the concrete that now becomes our hard reality.

You may have heard of someone in passing, who lost their child in an accident, through suicide, or maybe through an inevitable death from a disability which had affected the child since birth. Of course we feel sympathy: 'Oh my God, that's just awful, I am so sorry'. We might then desperately pray for our own luck, that we never have to feel this pain: and we may say, 'Thank God this has not happened to me; I couldn't cope with that.'

After a reflection, a pause, we decide that we must put it to the back of our minds, so that our imaginations aren't tortured by trying to understand how it actually feels. Then we move on with our lives...only glancing back every now and then, unable to imagine this: and so choosing not to.

I know this because I did this myself, before. I was too scared to believe that it could ever happen to me, unable to understand how anyone ever deals with this kind of loss. So we all tend to block these things from our minds, except to pass on our sympathies to the newly bereaved, and to remember their loved one with a sad face, and then perhaps to offer a few words of comfort when anniversaries come round.

I had heard of a couple of cases of at the same school that my girls went to: one through a road accident, one through cancer. In that awful moment, you are unable to understand the pain that the parent feels, so you don't try to force it: you don't claim to be able to understand, and you thank God once again that it wasn't your child.

In a way, you don't believe that things like that can ever happen to you. They only happen to other people; those in the news, or those you might hear about through friends. It would never happen to you. That is genuinely what you believe. And what I too once believed.

To talk about any kind of death, it seems, is so unnatural for this society in which we live, let alone the death of a child, at any age. Yet, it is one of the two things we all share: to be born and to die. I wonder why we are so scared of our own mortality, and why we are so reluctant to talk openly about such an inevitability?

I guess that I too had feared death; or that I had feared the lack of understanding around the fact that we don't know how long we have in this world, in this body. We hate to not have this control over ourselves. Is death pre-destined? Is it that we return to somewhere? What is this heaven that we learn about at such a young age? Across all religions and even from those with no religious beliefs, there seems to be a human need to construct the idea of heaven.

All these questions: and yet, not a huge amount of understanding. I remember after losing Liana, thinking, 'If she can die so courageously, then I can have no fear of death, now' – I guess that I feel a connection with 'the other side' now that is stronger than ever. I will touch on this later, in more detail.

Suddenly, my fear of death and dying had disappeared. Maybe it was that instant thought of, 'I can go where she is, any day' or, 'I won't be alone there, with her'? I don't know. It just felt different.

Finding Words

What do you say to someone who has lost a child, anyway? There is no rehearsal, no rule book. Nothing you could say that would give any comfort in such a huge event, so it is often easier to say nothing at all.

God forbid that you might be the person who makes the bereaved parent cry again, when crying is all they seem to do. You wouldn't dare to be the person to do that: that would be awful.

Maybe, a few weeks later, when you are walking through the shops, you see the bereaved parent in the distance, and you start to panic. 'Shit! I don't know what to do or say: what will they be like?' and so you quickly hide behind the jumper rack or cross the road and stare intently into a shop window, until you are sure that they have passed you by. Phew! you think – they didn't see you.

Except that they did: they were looking all around them, as their eyes never rest; and they are so anxious of mind that their eyes dart around looking at everything and everyone. They are scared that they have a big flashing neon sign on their head, saying, 'My child died: can you believe it? I don't know how I am walking around, either!'

By this time, though, they've seen enough friends cross the road and avoid that awkward conversation. In a way, it makes it easier for them, too; in fact, you couldn't add to their pain if you

135

tried. Nothing will ever hurt them more than that which they have already suffered, believe me.

It is quite possible that the sufferer has crossed the road to avoid you: to spare you the painful details, and to spare themselves from having to watch you being unsure of quite how to respond. Maybe they can't face telling the story again, being too exhausted by what is going through their minds to go into it yet again.

You hear of those suffering with cancer who sometimes say that people cross the road instead of speaking to them – and yep, it happens to bereaved parents, too! We don't have a warning sign, and yet we seem to stick out like a sore thumb. It's as though there is an invisible perimeter fence around us.

There are two sides to my grief as a mother, and it may be that other 'lost parents' can resonate with this. There is the grief that I show, and the grief that I feel. For me, those two areas of grief are so far apart, that I must describe them separately.

I became aware quite quickly after losing Liana that if I showed the grief that I really felt, in front of people, they wouldn't be able to cope with me. Close family and friends could, yes; but not people in my ordinary every-day life: the shop-keeper, the work colleague, the lady next door, friends of friends, etc. This is of course perfectly understandable: it is a private thing for both parties.

When I hollered out that pain, it scared me: so, it would sure as hell scare them. So, now as I write this, three years after Liana's death, I realise that there are two different ways in which I grieve.

The first way is the way that you will see if you should meet me on the street. The way in which I decide to show you that I can cope. The Mum who says things like:

'For Liana, twenty-two years were enough: she fought hard, but she had had enough,' or

'We were so lucky to have got the second chance of life, after her transplant: that was all she ever wanted, so we are grateful for that extra time,' or

'I will take on this pain as her Mum, as it means that she no longer has any pain.' (How bloody commendable!).

The second way is something so much more brutal and honest:

'I don't understand why I can't see her anymore: I need her, I miss her, my heart is screaming in pain, here,' or (especially at 3am):

'I can't find her! Why can't she just come home? I am meant to be able to look after her: I am her mother, so why would she leave me?' or even:

'I am not okay with this: I don't want to do this life without her; I can't do this, please don't make me do this; I can't hurt this much, please help me.'

I mean, which one could you deal with, coming face to face with me on the street?

I am aware that I would have very few people left in my circle if I behaved in the way that I really feel. I have already lost friends who could not cope with this grief; friends who have shown that they were only really friends if the story was about them: and by God, this really wasn't about them and their dramas. This was real life shit – heavy 'if you are going to stay friends with her, you need to be an extraordinary person' kind of shit: and they weren't: so I was happy to let them go. They stepped back, and I didn't grab hold: easily able to let them be released.

Isn't it funny how people whom I never knew that well could step forward and become the most incredible 'scaffolding' to support me? Others, some even in my closest circle, still made it all about them, and pulled back when they realised that nobody was interested in the minutiae of their lives anymore, because there was too much other stuff that needed to be dealt with! You never know who will pull you through this sort of situation until you have no choice left but to find out.

Then, of course, there were those who were desperate to be apart of a big story like Liana's. People who hadn't given a hoot about her when she was alive, had never visited her in hospital, and never reached out to her. Yet some started writing heaps of sentimental twaddle on social media about how one of their 'best friends had just died', and how they were 'devastated at their loss' – reeling in a big fat dish of responses such as, 'Ooh sweetie, I am so sorry for your loss', etc. Er, hello? You hadn't spoken with Liana in five years, and had never actually got on: and, believe me, she didn't like you, either...

This made me feel particularly wretched. I decided that I had to believe that this would have made her laugh out loud, had she been witness to it: that is how I would cope with them...

She would have written, had her angel wings been able to type, 'Are you effing kidding me? You're crazy: you always ignored me, we never got on, so who are you kidding?' I know this to be true! And it allows me to not 'let rip' out loud.

Those who really knew Liana could hear her say that, just then, reading it from this page: go on! – yes, you could!

Rant over... I have to say that Facebook and the like allowed those who genuinely cared to keep up to date with us, support us, be with us when we lived in hospital, when we were in Kenya, when she got her second chance at life.

It was overwhelming just how much love you could feel by glancing at your phone. I never got tired of it, it was always welcome, it was always needed. It's a funny old world.

Social media was a particularly good thing, when Liana was ill: and yes, even when she had died. It had enabled her to stay in touch with those she loved, and with those with whom she had had a relationship. It was social media that had allowed forty messages of love and support during each day that she was on life-support for the final time, and that had allowed me to be held together when I was seriously frayed at the edges.

It was a connection, and it still is. It was a fundraiser, and indeed it still is, in her memory. It provided a remarkable stream of love, and it still does to this day. The outpouring of love that I get from those whom I care about is a total blessing. If you have been a part of that, then I thank you so much: I really do.

The Gaping Hole

It is an agony and it is harrowing.

It's as though my heart fell out of my chest, that day; and all these lovely people are now around me, just pushing a little bit of it back into my chest wall when it pops out too far. It will always be exposed, it will never heal fully; it can't: but it can be helped back in a little, when the hurt is too much to bear.

Gentle words from others add a small patch to the gaping hole in my chest. Loving hugs, beautiful messages; all of these can hold a sticking plaster over the open wound for a little while. I am continually searching for little sticking plasters, reasons for my heart to not be slopped all over the floor in an ugly mess, bruised, pale and totally broken.

After the loss of a child, other losses are diminished. I couldn't understand how I could lose my lovely Dad, just two years after losing Liana, and not experience the same level of grief.

Of course, I was dreadfully upset when Jay & Caitlin found my dear Dad at his home, having passed away during the night. I cried on my way home to Yeovil from Northampton, where I was at a training meeting for work. I woke up the next day and got teary when my Mum arrived, and we chatted: and I cried a little whilst reading my Dad's eulogy at his funeral. Otherwise, I have not been able to cry. It frustrates me, and it disappoints me that I cannot cry at losing him. My sister cries about him each time we meet, but I do not. I see other people's grief at losing a parent, but sadly I cannot deal with my own. I can't allow myself to start this process again.

This distresses me, of course. It feels as though it shows a lack of respect that I can't grieve more for the loss of his huge presence in my life. I miss him and his love. I miss going to visit him: he lived alone, and it was always a help to him that I could wash and change his bedding and do some housework for him. Sometimes, he would let me sit and just cry about Liana. His words of comfort, in his understanding of our shared grief, were never judgmental, and never anything but loving. Yet, I cannot cry at losing him? He was my lovely Papa! My safe place. It seems surreal that I can even sit and type the words, 'I cannot grieve for him.'

Or maybe I do cry; but as soon as I cry about anything, it all goes back to one thing: Liana. It was explained to me by a friend at the bereavement support group that I go to once a month, like this...

When you open your filing cabinet of grief, out of all the files that it contains, the one called 'Grief for Liana' is so BIG that this file is the one that jumps up in front of you, and makes all others seem smaller in comparison: so, you grieve for HER all over again.

This is true: and it is a very helpful way by which to try to understand my feelings. I was grateful to have this analogy shared with me, as it lessens my guilt, more than a little. I am trying to keep my filing cabinet locked, when it comes to other grief: as I know exactly what will happen if I dare to open it.

Sometimes, it springs open with little warning, and then boom! – there she is again... Always Liana.

It's hard to see that others grieve so hard for their lost parents, and that I apparently cope so well with it, myself. It's not that I am okay about the fact that Dad died: but that I am possibly too scared to keep that filing cabinet open for very long, and to have to then start to confront yet another grief.

Going to my monthly parent bereavement group is incredibly helpful. It is the place where we can feel no envy, only compassion; no competition, only understanding. We can all laugh, or we can all cry: nothing seems to be out of bounds or off limits, and we all know that we couldn't hurt each other any more than we already hurt: so there is a certain kind of freedom and understanding in our conversations that we are unable to find elsewhere.

We ask the questions which nobody ever seems to ask. How did your son/daughter die? What did you do on your first Christmas without them? How do you go on working? How did it affect your marriage? Literally nothing seems to be out of bounds. It is a safe place to be.

This is a group that not one of us asked to join. Each time we meet, it is a remarkable thing to be able to help others: to get things off your chest, to feel united by grief, and to always know that this is actually okay. No explanations are needed.

We totally understand what it is like to be near a bereaved parent, and to not have a clue what to say to them: remember that we haven't always been afflicted by this role.

What do you say to a bereaved parent? Perhaps we should start with what NOT to say. I know that the worst thing that you can say to me – and yes, it has been said all too many times – is, 'I didn't come over, as I didn't know what to say to you' – (Oh, okay then!) – and two people actually said to me, 'I'm sorry I didn't come to Liana's funeral: I'm not good with funerals, as I find them too difficult!' – Oh, okay, did you think that I wanted to be there? Did you think that I was in it for the fun? Jesus, well there you go, then – you pretty much didn't see outside of yourself there then, did you!

So, the best thing you can say to a bereaved parent?

'Tell me about …*name*: I'd love to know what you remember about her when she was being funny?'

'Tell me about what …*name* liked most about Christmas.'

'Tell me – do you need any support? And is there something I can do that would help you?'

'I'd love to tell you something I remember about …*name*.'

Grab all your courage with both hands, walk up to that parent and just say, 'Hi'.

You cannot say the wrong thing: saying nothing is worse than saying the wrong thing. Saying, 'I'm sorry to hear your news,' isn't going to make them realise that their child has died. You needn't worry about reminding them of it, because it is the most prominent thing in their life – for the rest of their life.

144

If they don't want to talk they will tell you, without being unkind, that they don't want to right now. Don't be offended by that: be pleased that they can be honest with you, to spare themselves a little more pain. Just make sure that they know that you are always there for them, if and when they might need to talk to someone.

Even when I laugh the hardest, there is a tugging somewhere in my heart. When I breathe in a zest for life and feel genuine joy, there is still that tugging somewhere in my heart. You can't say what it is: you just know it's there. Invisible, yet undeniable.

Something is wrong: sometimes I can't even put my finger on what is wrong with me. I may feel grumpy or sad or prickly and edgy, and will say to Jay or to a friend, 'I don't know what's wrong with me today' – and they'll say, 'Really? Hmm, let me see, you lost your child: that's what is wrong, and it's okay for you to feel like this today and every day!'

I know that my true friends look at me and know exactly what I face, each day: they tell me they know – they forgive me every failing that I have as a friend, every tough time, and every middle-of-the-night text telling them that I can't do this without her, anymore...

Needing Support

Where do you find support when you have lost a child? I felt that there was support out there if you lost someone to cancer or similar, but that there is only a very limited amount of help and support if you have lost a child. I may be wrong. It was purely by chance that a friend of a friend told me about the local parent bereavement support group where I have found so much support.

Perhaps you couldn't cope with sharing emotions or thoughts in this way? I know people who have lost a child and who couldn't face going to a support group like mine. But every bereaved parent should know about the networks that exist, and be given information by doctors, hospitals, social workers, etc. There are now many kinds of support to help bereaved people with all the very painful issues around their grief.

We need to talk about it more, and not hide behind our fears of upsetting someone. We were allowed to leave the hospital, after Liana had passed away, without being given any helpful contact numbers, or any information about where to look for much-needed emotional and practical support following our very sad loss.

Losing a child is a different kind of grief. Other grief often, hopefully, gets gently smaller as time passes. Maybe it takes a long time or a short time, but generally you can accept loss a little more easily when the person is older: a different generation, a grandparent, a parent, an elder.

The grief that comes with losing a child stays the same size: it is simply that you learn to grow bigger around it. That is how it feels to me.

You see, the problem that I have here is that, as a parent, as Liana's Mum, and as Caitlin's Mum, I have always needed to know (pretty much) that they are okay. Did their flight land safely? Did they get through the floods in their car? Did their dental appointment go well? Did they get rid of their headache? This is a major problem when the child has died, of course: but you still need to know the answer to the question, 'Are you okay?'

The feeling doesn't go away just because they have died. In fact, the realisation that if they are not okay, then you can do NOTHING to help them, is even more debilitating. You need to know. You will now never know. Your yearning for them and your link to them is never broken, even by death. So, you never stop worrying.

I can understand that at the point of realising that Liana was not likely to make it through this last round of life-support, I begged her to let go: to leave this awful, painful body behind her, and to go and be at rest, and have peace. 'I promise you that I will be okay,' I said, 'It's okay to leave and be free, darling,' I said. That is what we know: that is how we know it to be true; but I can't tell you that I don't panic at times about how she is, even though she is in heaven!

I don't know how, or if, you can let go of that maternal instinct that comes into play the second

148

that they are born. It hasn't left me yet, and I can assure you that it never will. I will always feel that I should have done more.

As a parent, aren't you meant to be able to fix things when they go wrong with your child? They fall over and bang their knee, you pick them up and put a plaster on it, and you kiss them better. They are sick in the night, and you sit with them, hold them and reassure them. But this was a situation which was totally out of our control. I couldn't fix this one if I'd spent the rest of my life trying: and I would have kept trying, except that this particular state of affairs had sadly left me absolutely powerless to help Liana.

Although I had tried to be a kidney donor to her, I was not a match: that was a whole different acute disappointment. I did join the pairing scheme database, after rigorous testing, to allow me to donate to another person in return for Liana finding a match; but we didn't get this chance, as she got her donor match before we were able to be paired. But to be honest, I would have given my life to spare hers: yet even this was not possible.

I wrote this next paragraph on the notes page in my phone about a year after Liana died. I was travelling, and this is what came to my mind at that time, it is the foreward to this book and I feel it is appropriate to include it again here:

"When you have a child, I guess you know there will be moments that are difficult. Sometimes parents will find themselves in a situation that they never anticipated, and there's always a deep instinct to protect your child.

When the situation calls for it and a parent must do the thing that they never thought possible, letting their child go, it is the betrayal of all things normal. There is no 'way' for it to happen that makes it okay; it will never be okay: so how does your heart find the strength to keep beating?

'It's not your story!' are four words that Liana said to me, early in her journey, that she maybe knew, maybe not, would be one of the reasons I am able to continue my own journey It was when someone suggested I write about her story, as I had a history of working in publishing, that she leapt up and yelled, 'It's not your story!' At that moment I realised that the feeling we get when we become parents is of an 'ownership' of our children: that they belong to us, and it is up to us to ensure their future, their safety, their life. We forget that our life and story belong to us, and not to our parents. So then, for our children, the story of their life belongs to them.

Of course we try to shape them and teach them right from wrong. But we cannot change their story and we can't stop them from leaving us when their time here is done.

Their story is only a part of us, and doesn't belong to us. 'It's not your story!' – so then we must find the strength to let go of our guilt, our anger, and our frustration. We cannot get rid of our pain, but we can try and rise above some of the other pressures that we feel around our loss."

So, we need to remember that WE didn't fail, and we couldn't stop it: honestly, we couldn't. Or we would have, a million times over: we would have!

What about losing another child? So, you think lightning doesn't strike twice? You can't tell that to a parent who has lost a child – no way. If they have lost one, they can go on and lose the rest. They know the feeling now, and they fear it happening again. You can't persuade them otherwise. In fact, I know of two people in my own circle of bereaved parents who had lost both their children from different causes and at different times. I do not know how I would cope with this; in the same way in which a parent with all their children still living can't imagine losing one. So, now this is my new prayer. My new unimaginable thing.

...

The first year is 'different' – I thought that it would be the worst. Maybe it was the most raw? The toughest? But, not the worst...

I felt as though I had been a ball-bearing, slung out into a pinball machine with no warning from behind; just pinging from one side to the next, all over the place, going off like a rocket but having no control: not knowing what the next assault on your heart would be, and then, 'Ping!' – you are slammed against another pain. It was crazy.

I understood what people meant when they said that it was as though your head was in a goldfish bowl. I could see everything around me, and I could hear it all; but there was something stopping me from taking anything in. I was in my own petrifying place, inside this bowl.

Things were echoed, strange, and slow moving –
and yet my head wouldn't shut up. It wouldn't stop
thinking a hundred things a second, so didn't that
make it feel too fast? How is fast slow? It didn't make
sense. I didn't understand it, and I certainly didn't
want it: it wasn't real, but a dream, a nightmare: and
every day seemed to last for too long, and I wanted
to just sleep so that I could shut up the noise in my
head.

Sleeping tablets, that had worked before, did
nothing but make me feel drunk and woozy; I liked
that, though: anything other than the alert and angry
pain. I would still wake up throughout the night and
would find myself wandering around the house whilst
everyone else slept. I'd sit and stare out of the window,
just trying to contemplate the last few years. The
realisation of what had happened. In disbelief, I guess.

I wanted my head to shut up torturing me. I
wanted it all to stop, and to just be able to step off the
world for a while: perhaps to come back later, when
some of the pain had diminished? Apparently, that
can't happen.

Waking up in the morning was often the hardest,
as consciousness brought the daily crushing
realisation of what had been lost, new and raw again,
each day.

At intermittent times throughout each day I would
realise all over again, as though she had only just
died, that she was gone: and it would all come
crashing down. It was totally unbearable, and it
didn't seem to have an end date either, which was
frightening.

Realisations such as, 'Oh, it's true – she's not actually coming back,' do still happen, and often; but during the first year they were ten a penny: too often, and too painful. You are just trying to wade through life as though you are trying to walk through a river of treacle.

There is the grief of realising that there are so many people now who will never know her. Caitlin's children will never have their Auntie Liana: to them she will be a lady that their Mum and their Nanna talk about, and they will see the photos that we have around; but it breaks my heart to think that they won't hold her, too. They won't catch her infectious giggles; she would have got them into trouble being naughty, just to annoy their Mum, her sister: believe me, she would have done that!

In her absence, life will go on. Life is going on. Though without her in it. She is, instead, a beautiful memory. She will never get old, she will always be young and beautiful. She has now become a part of a time in so many people's lives that they have tucked away in their hearts, and they remember often, removing anything except love for her.

Sadness can be too much for a person to bear. It is too much for a parent to bear when they grieve for a child. There is something there tugging at your heart every day: a heap of reminders, a hundred thoughts, some regrets, some emotion, some anger, and frustration.

You say to yourself, she would have loved that dress in the window. She would have screamed with laughter at that joke. She would have looked beautiful in any wedding dress. She would have made him turn his head. She would have lived each moment as though it was her last. Except that all of this now just happens in my head. And it keeps her alive: knowing where she would have been, what she would have done, how it would have been.

You see, just because she is not here, it doesn't mean that I wouldn't be able to imagine. I knew her well enough that often I hear exactly the words that would have come out of her mouth. The link is never really broken. I will always keep it alive. I may not see her, but I feel her...

Remembering You

What you're left with when your child passes away, aside from the grief, the physical belongings, and the pain, are memories. Except that you stumble to find them through the tears and the heartbreak.

What became clear to me, after losing Liana, was that hearing memories from all those who had known her painted a picture of her life which was even richer than the one which I had thought was already pretty full.

I took comfort in others' memories, and in their impressions of her. To watch their faces, as they remembered her, brought me even more love and pride for her, could that have been possible.

Then, as my own head started to allow me to think even half straight about my personal memories of precious moments, I realised that I, too, could see through my pain: and could bring back to my mind things that not only made me cry for my loss, but that also made me laugh, too – sometimes hysterically!

About a year after our loss, I wanted to start documenting these memories to revisit them at a later time. Not just to keep her alive, but also to remember them during times of reflection, and at times when I needed to turn my agony around. When sometimes the pain becomes too much, with that tsunami that takes your legs from under you, it's okay to try and find a way back with these special memories.

I hope that these suggestions will allow you to find some direction in your time of grief, and that they will help you to start to remember and document precious conversations, comments, thoughts and memories of your own...

My Child:

Why we chose your name...
The first time I saw you...
The feeling of love for you is like...
Your first home...
What I was most proud of...
Your young personality...
Why you loved Christmas...
Your eyes...
Your smile...
Distinctive features...
When you laughed...
Your dislikes...
Best family holidays...
Your strengths...
Your impact on others...
What your friends share with me about you...

What Matters

I know that Liana's work with organ donation was desperately important to her. She always wanted to ensure that people got that second chance at life if they needed it. It is another area we don't talk about enough with our loved ones, but it is vitally important. Believe me, you don't need it when you're gone, and you're not coming back to this body, ever!

I find it incredible that so many people choose not to donate their organs when they die, but that if they themselves needed an organ donation to stay alive, they would then take one! But, I guess that until you are in that situation, you will never know how you will react, or what your family will do on your behalf.

Education is needed to remove both fear and misguided information. Do you really think that a doctor will pretend that you are brain-dead, just to get an organ donation for another human being? I have actually heard people say, 'What if I am not really dead?' A doctor will only ever want to save lives – YOUR LIFE – and then, if that isn't possible, to give another who is struggling a chance to survive.

If I could bottle the feeling that I got when Liana received her second chance at life and then show it to you, I would. It would change your life, too. The overwhelming gratitude, love, pride, raw emotion, hope and relief. If it were a colour, it would overwhelm you with its beauty – a colour you've never seen before. Think of that feeling as a child on Christmas morning and multiply it by a trillion times, and you will still come up short. It makes you value life as you have never done before. It makes you love harder and stronger. It makes you grateful for the small things.

It makes you realise that people matter. Nothing else, except people. Not where you live, or how much you earn. Liana didn't lie on her bed, in those final hours, panicking that she only had a little, battered red Ford KA on the driveway and not a Porsche!

All that mattered to her in those last moments were the people who surrounded her and all the love that was pushed into her soul. The memories. The laughter. The happy times. The joy of friends and of love.

She wouldn't have looked back and thought, 'I really wish I'd had a Porsche,'... I promise you.

I feel blessed to understand that, now. Having spent years trying my hardest to be the most successful that I could be in my work, often at the expense of my family and friends, I see now that where I live and what I look like doesn't matter to those who love me.

Okay, I still wear make-up and do my hair, so there is an element of caring about what I look like: but will it kill me not to have it? Will I be less of a person without a Porsche? Will I be looked down upon if I don't work twelve-hour days?

I understand it, now. What can we learn that opens our eyes? What becomes clearer through our loss? What is important, now?

I am grateful to have been taught this, through the loss of my child. I look back at Liana's life and I only really need to remember how much love she shared. How wonderful she smelt in her favourite perfume (I still have the bottle, and sometimes just close my eyes and breathe her in). How funny she was. How slightly crazy she was. How many times we said, 'I love you'. How much passion she had for organ donation. How much she loved being with her friends. How much life she had in her, right until the end.

I wish I had understood some of these things earlier, to know how to look at the blue sky and see its beauty and feel grateful. My new knowledge allows me to breathe in, sit back and appreciate the tiniest of things. It makes me laugh louder, love harder.

Sometimes, people have said to me: 'I don't know how you get up each day; I don't know how you do it.' I always reply, 'I have no choice: the other option would be to lie in bed crying and heartbroken. But I cannot do that. I have to get up every day, fight back and enjoy each day that I am given, because the arrival of a new day should never be taken for granted. So I get up, I put on my war paint, and I live another day.' Just one day at a time.

I know that if I were to lie in bed and give up, I would be letting Liana down. If she were here, she would be giving life 100%: even at the times when she only felt like 60%, she was an all or nothing kind of girl. I want to be like her. I want to take whatever life throws my way, and suck it up and be glad that I have the chance to experience such things.

Would lying in bed crying not hurt more than this life I choose to take part in? It scares me to think about that option more so funnily enough.

Don't get me wrong: life is not a bed of roses; we still must pay the bills, and do the housework and crappy things like that, but I am grateful that I have these choices, these chances. I don't get so down about trivial things anymore. Or maybe I do, but then something jolts me (she gives me a kick up the ass!) and I move forward again: happy, grateful, and more loving, more understanding.

She has, in her passing, opened a whole world of understanding for me. I can't stand it when I hear people moan about their hard luck, and about how tough life is. How sorry they feel for themselves that they must work so hard, or feel that they are unlucky because they can't have a holiday this year! I don't say anything: but it is quite clear that they don't feel satisfied by their lives, and this is such a waste of life. I don't do that anymore.

Maybe Liana really knew all along that her life would be short – because she ate the cake, she broke the rules, she laughed intensely, she loved truly, and she had absolutely no regrets. I guess that she went out kicking and screaming and with her hands in the air, saying, 'Woohoo! I enjoyed the ride!' – so this is how I choose to remember her.

Living with you right beside me still, sweetie.

From Liana

*Whilst sat in hospital I decided today was the day...
time to finally start writing a blog.*

*I've always been told by so many people that I should
write down my story for people to read. It has occurred
to me that maybe by sharing my story and experiences
through a blog I could hopefully inspire more people to
join the Organ Donor Register. Here goes...*

*It all started in 2010 when I suffered an allergic
reaction to my anti-malaria tablet, Doxycycline, whilst
teaching in Uganda, Africa. It caused my pancreas
to haemorrhage and fail which then led to both of
my kidneys to fail. My organs were shutting down
and I was fighting against the odds in the middle of
nowhere!*

*I was flown to Nairobi, Kenya for urgent treatment
but was not expected to make it. An amazing team
of doctors managed to keep me alive and after a
couple of weeks in ICU I was well enough to be taken
back to hospital in the UK. Unfortunately, my multiple
organ failure went from acute to chronic, leading me
to spend the next 2 years living in hospital (escaping
when possible). I was surviving the renal failure by
having haemodialysis 3x weekly 3-4hrs each time.*

*Due to severe pain in my stomach when I ate
(chronic pancreatitis), I was unable to eat for a long*

time and developed an eating disorder, where I associated food with pain. I went through a stage of heavy depression that lasted what felt like a lifetime. The life I had once lived was gone forever.

I had to undergo various surgeries both minor and major, resulting in the majority of my pancreas being taken out in London, along with my gallbladder being removed in Bristol and a long list of infections.

After these rocky couple of years I was stable enough to be able to visit friends and home and have more freedom. I had help with my depression through medication and various therapies, and I can proudly say I conquered my eating disorder and found my love for food...and life. I started doing whatever I physically could to live my life as 'normal' as possible.

I was finally well enough to be put on the transplant waiting list!! On January 28th 2014, After years waiting, I received 'the call'. The transplant operation was a complete success and the kidney started to work before they closed me up!

I am now on my next chapter... My second chance at life.

Liana xoxo

Happiness Still Happens

It occurred to me whilst writing this book that there is another story that needs to be told. There is still so much happiness in my life.

Quote me: "I am often the happiest I have ever been."

Isn't that something you didn't think you would hear from a bereaved parent?

Through the dreadful loss of a child, my child, at such a young age and after such a brutal and lengthy illness, you surely can't come out the other side feeling happier than you were before you went in?

Yet, I have...

Of course, there are times (many) that I can be found on the floor in a heap, sobbing uncontrollably. Unable to stop the pain as it rips through me, of course that still happens. It petrifies me each time that I can hurt that much; but it is because of what we went through that allows me to feel genuine happiness.

I am grateful for each day that I wake up. I am aware that others don't wake up, on this day. I am stronger, I care more, I laugh more: I find more joy than I have known before.

I look and see the beauty of the sky – only because I have witnessed the ugliness of such pain. I feel and appreciate each hug I receive more – only because I long to hug her. I understand what absolute love is – only because I was taught it even more than I realised I knew, when I lost it. I know how to laugh so much that it physically hurts my belly – because of the amount of real hurt that I feel there, too.

How can I ever feel so good? Because I know what it is to feel so bad.

I am grateful for the lessons that I have been taught. I no longer fear death. I am less precious about things. You need money? I will give it to you, if I have it. You want a holiday? I will take it with you right NOW, because we may not get the chance again. You think about doing something? I do something – and with urgency. Do now, think later.

I am not better than you: I am now just different from you.

I allow myself, mostly, to get over the small stuff and see only the greatest things. I don't moan about the rain – I am amazed at how it feeds this Earth. I don't hide from a lightning storm – I am excited to see its beauty.

I holiday with friends, and drink in the fun. I eat the cake (well the gluten-free cake, anyway!), although I do still moan that my backside is too fat (but how is that important, eh?!). I want to be part of my friends' lives more. I love sharing good times with those I care about, because I care about them more than I ever used to... Even more than that!

I can do all of this because I don't feel that Liana is missing out. I knew her so well that I can tell you just where she would be sitting at a party, what she would be wearing to the celebrations I attend, and how much fun she would have had on the holiday. I could have told you that she would have been the centre of attention at my wedding to Jay, two and a half years after her passing.

Of course, these feelings were not present at the beginning.

I thought that when you lost your child, you would stay in bed for three months, crying, in pain, and unable to function. I know bereaved parents who have done exactly that. I could have done that. I chose not to. Doing that scares me even more than living without her. It is somehow (and I don't know how) easier for me to live a happy life, and to be positive, than it is to curl up and die.

Liana wouldn't want that. I know that she wants me to be happy. I know that she wants me to feel alive. I know that, because she told me so. She told me that I had no choice but to live without her. She gave me my orders. I had to stay alive and strong: and all she cared about was that I was going to look after Caitlin. I hope that this is exactly what I do. I can honour Liana's memory in that way, by not giving up.

Every time I laugh, she would be proud. Every time I smile, she would be glad: and I truly believe that she is out there somewhere in her spiritual form, knowing that I am doing okay.

I must believe this.

The first time that I experienced events after her death, it was agony. The family meal she didn't attend. A friend of hers getting married or having a baby that she didn't see. All of it hurt. In fact, it hurt so much that I would sit, sobbing. I do still always cry at times when the whole extended family is together, because her void is so much larger then. I realised that I couldn't continue to do this, and it was because I felt so close to her that she would be right there with me at all these times.

That had to give me peace... So, now I tell myself, 'She would have loved this, and she is probably here with us, right now, having fun anyway'; and it allows me to take enjoyment, instead of dreading things. I have learned too many times now that I worry more leading up to the event without her, than at the actual event without her!

Our wedding was the largest gathering that I'd had to plan without her, and there were times when it felt wrong; of course there were. But, the day was about us, it wasn't about Liana; and when a friend reminded me of this, things seemed to get easier – much easier.

I had tried so hard to include her everywhere in the wedding, at the beginning; and I had thought of so much: but on the day itself, I had made peace with it and I didn't want this inclusion to be overwhelming, either for us or for any of our guests.

I had arranged that an empty chair would be saved for her, next to the bridesmaids in the front row: but then, closer to the day, I realised that I didn't want to turn around and see an empty chair there, right beside me, reminding me of her obvious absence: so, I didn't do it.

I had asked a friend, who had known her so very well, to represent Liana at the wedding: and I'd asked her to do a reading that included Liana, and that talked about her: but when it came to it, and rightly so, she gently told me that her talk was going to be about 'us' and about 'love'; and that nobody wanted to get upset, missing Liana in that moment: she was very honest. Thank God that she could see past our pain – and that she could then move us all on, towards what was right.

I had written a poem on a chalk board to display at the wedding, but I left it at home and nobody got to see it. So, for the first time, here it is:

Our Liana

Your picture in my flowers
We saved you your own chair
To be with us right at the front
We know that you'll be there
We guess that you'll be smiling
You may even shed a tear
Now you can be just anywhere
We know that you'll choose here
We love you with our hearts
And miss you even more
But we still believe and say
When we are three, we are still four

It took a while for me to ask my friends to walk with me down the aisle. At first, I just wanted Caitlin, who was giving me away, to walk with me. My Dad was too disabled physically to ask him, really (and sadly, he then passed away just four months before our wedding), but I really wanted Caitlin to do it from the outset, as it felt special and right.

I was worried at first that if I asked anyone else to walk with me, I would feel as though I was 'replacing' Liana, as I had always dreamed of both of my girls walking with me towards Jay. Then, as the weeks went by, it dawned on me that I wanted my friends to walk with me on this very special day, because they walked with me every day. They always stood by me, so why would that day be any different?

So, I 'popped the question' over a drink one evening at the pub. It was fun! – and we all laughed and got even more excited at the prospect of all being together on the day.

A lovely way to bring Liana into it was for each of them, and Caitlin, to carry a little wooden heart in their flowers, each with one of Liana's initials on them, so that when they stood together it spelt her name.

I was totally engaged in the preparations for the big day – and I realised, on a few occasions, how happy I was to be able to feel again. It was great to have something wonderful for everyone to celebrate together: and we really wanted it to be about our closest family and friends being together, without it being a flipping funeral! We had had so many of those in the previous two years that it was time to celebrate something happy.

The day before the wedding, I went up to Liana's grave and sat awhile in contemplation. Of course I did. But, not for long. Just long enough to sit and tell her that I knew that she would be there with me on our wedding day. I left her some flowers that I had also used in my wedding bouquet, and I knew that I felt better for doing this.

I thought to myself how she would be saying, 'Well you can carry on and sit up there – I'm off to the wedding venue to have some fun!' – so I knew that she wouldn't want me to be sitting there for very long, if at all...

Then the chaos and the fun began: the dress was collected, the bridesmaids and friends gathered, and we all went over to the wedding venue to dress it, ready for the next day.

We had taken over a beautiful country house hotel for the weekend and had allocated all twenty-one guest rooms to our family and friends. It was a wonderfully romantic venue, and I guess that I had chosen it (and had also persuaded Jay that this was the place) because I had shared many happy memories there with Liana, using the spa and the grounds for afternoon tea with her.

I had spent so long making tulle pom-poms that I had considered starting a business! 'Deck the halls' we did, and it was such an exciting day. Jay left in the evening: and after some food, my female friends and I were spending the night before the big day there. Caitlin and I shared a suite, and all the girls piled in there together for a while – we were all there in our pyjamas, with glasses of bubbly and lots of laughter!

My bridesmaids had all put their resources together, and they gave me some beautiful gifts that night, all presented in a lovely personalised box. When I lifted the lid, there were lots of photos of us all together – and many of them included fun times with Liana, too. She was there – they made sure of that.

It was easy to be happy, and as I look back now on that day I realise that I never once felt sad that Liana wasn't there. I gave myself permission to really enjoy it all, and I did.

Liana wasn't missing, walking down the aisle: Caitlin took the role with pride and love, and it felt okay; it felt perfect. We were a team of two who had come through the roughest years together – and we walked this together as a duo, too!

I felt incredibly happy, and loved and, as I walked down the aisle, our guests were streaming with tears, pretty much all of them. It just felt okay to be happy. I had never been this happy.

Liana, whilst always in my thoughts, did not overwhelm my mind or upset me at all on that day. We didn't need to declare how much we loved her. Everyone there already knew this, which consequently gave us permission to just 'be happy'.

This was very empowering in my grief journey. I feel very lucky to have had such a wonderful experience after such pain. It allowed me to realise even more deeply how important it is to move forward.

My Spiritual Feelings

I have always been spiritual in my beliefs. Whilst not being a traditional church-goer, it seems that I was religious enough to find the chapel in every hospital and to spend time praying!

My personal feelings, and I know that they are only mine and do not belong to others, are that we are here on a journey to learn and to teach. I believe that we are here on this Earth possibly many times, in whichever role that we need to learn from.

The after-life, as a spiritualist believes, is a place where one continues to evolve; and my interaction with spiritualist mediums has been a large part of my life. I also believe that we all can connect with the spirit, and that we can learn and develop these abilities through practice.

Maybe this part of the book doesn't interest you, and that is okay. I would be denying others, who know how I feel, not to add this dimension to my story, and to Liana's story; as spiritualism has played such a huge part in our lives, and in my understanding of her death.

Liana used to come with me often to the spiritualist church in Yeovil. We both shared a belief in 'life after death from this body', and we felt sure that the spirit moved on from this Earthly realm. We spoke openly together about this belief, many times, and especially so as she was so sick.

I know she wasn't scared of dying: she told me. She was only scared of pain, and she often said that she felt that death would have been easier than what she was going through. I too often used to wonder if it would have been kinder to her if she had passed away in Kenya, and had not then had to endure such agony. It felt so wrong to feel that way, but I can't lie: I did feel that way, and often!

There was definitely a moment of 'release' involved in her death, and I am sure that I felt it, even as she passed. No more pain, no more fear. I think most parents feel that they would do anything to keep their child; however this is not the case if the child's life will be full of pain and suffering.

I still say that you wouldn't let a dog live with the pain that she had had: you would put it to sleep, kindly, putting an end to its suffering. Yet here we were, month after month, year after year, watching her pain being endured both physically and mentally. So, death was indeed a release for her.

We had a deal: when she died, she would show me that she was still there. And she did, on her terms, of course. In fact, very quickly – and just two days after she died, when I was upstairs on the landing, and crying to my friends that I couldn't feel her. This was prompted by Caitlin saying that when she had woken up that day she could feel Liana with her. I was jealous, and wondering, 'Why can't I feel her?' Jay and my friends lifted me up from the floor, and got me into the shower...

I cried into the water, absolutely sobbing – and then it happened. The water stopped. I stood for a moment trying to work out who had turned it off, and I looked up at the shower head and, 'whoosh!' – there it was, freezing cold water right in my face!

I yelled out at the cold, leapt out of the shower and ran into the bedroom – where my friends had been anxiously waiting for me to shower, and had been there to keep an eye on me. 'She's here! I feel her!', I cried.

It was later during that day that I got the absolute confirmation that I needed of her presence. A couple of hours later, I realised that I had left my watch upstairs in the bathroom. As I placed it back on my wrist, I was confused by the time that it read. I knew that it was mid-afternoon, but it said 12.15pm on the dial. It was a beautiful watch that Jay had bought me some years before, and it had never failed – so I moved it on to the correct time and went downstairs. As I did so, I asked a friend, 'At what time was I in the shower?' Her reply of confirmation, 'At about twelve-fifteen' was incredible!

As I looked at my watch and realised that it was ticking along nicely again, I took that as another sign that she was with me in the bathroom in that moment. The watch still works well to this day, and it has never stopped since then!

Sign number three that day came as I stood in the kitchen with Nicky, having the fiftieth cry of the day – and my first white feather appeared, right there on the floor beside us.

Thank you, Liana...

I keep that feather, and others, in a bottle on the kitchen window-sill. In fact, it is the large drinking bottle that Liana carried with her after her transplant, due to the volume of water that she had to drink each day. It has since had many white feathers placed inside it...

I know when she is near me. This is also made clearer to me because I also know when she is not! Some of the signs that I get are obvious, and they are ones that most people have heard mentioned before; others are very personal: a feeling, or perhaps a signal, that only could have meant something to her.

Our friends, who had stayed with us after her death, eventually had to leave and go back to their normal lives. I was extremely anxious about us being on our own, as three – as it was easier to have a house full of people than to have it as just 'us', making it blatantly obvious that Liana was the one missing. As they left, the house seemed very quiet for the first time in over a week. It was just the three of us, or so we thought. Jay, Caitlin and I sat in silence for a moment in the living room, and that silence was suddenly shattered when a picture of Liana fell forward on the sideboard!!

The picture was leaning backwards on its stand, so it would have been impossible for it to fall forward without help. I think that this was the point at which Caitlin screamed, and then jumped onto the sofa next to me! I laughed hard, and I felt that Liana was making sure that we realised that we were not alone. Therefore, we always now say, 'When we are three, we are still four.' Liana would not want to be missing out!

Thank you, Liana...

White feathers do appear in the most random of places. I have felt her sitting next to me in the car on a long journey. It happened on my way back from work in Northampton one afternoon, and I couldn't get her out of my mind. It was about six months after she had died, and she was really stuck in my head. I knew that she was there, so I put out my hand, palm facing up, and just said quietly, 'I love you, sweetie.' My hand started to warm up, and I just felt incredibly peaceful.

I stopped for fuel at the next service station; and there it was, when I got back into my car – there was a white feather on the dashboard! I started laughing. You couldn't make it up!

Thank you, Liana.

We were given many messages of validation over the coming months. On one occasion, a friend of a friend had been at an evening event with a local psychic medium. Although she hadn't known Liana very well, she was told that Liana was there, trying to get a message through. The medium told my acquaintance about the girl who had been to Africa; that she was there, and that she was saying another friend's name. That friend was able to come to me and tell me that Liana had come through to her with love.

This medium was well known locally, and so of course I booked to see her. It was a few months later when I got to visit her; as I hadn't met her before, I was excited to see if I could get real validation. I did.

When we sat together, the first thing she told me was that when I had arrived, and she had opened

the door, a voice had said in her mind, 'This is my
Mum – ask her why she is so strong?' – and then she
went on to tell me so many wonderful things, and
things that only Liana would know. She was telling
me about Liana's illness and her transplant - how she
had had enough of fighting, and how I had made the
right decision to let her go. It was a very exciting
connection.

She also told me that Liana knew that I had some
of her hair: this was kept in a special box alongside
some other precious things, which included a
gold ring that I had bought for Liana with the word
'survivor' engraved on it. She was correct. On Liana's
23rd birthday, the first one after her death, my Mum
had given me a beautiful organza bag full of Liana's
hair. When aged about fourteen, Liana had had her
long hair cut and given some to my mother, knowing
that she used felted fibres in her artwork. Liana had
asked her Gran to use it to make her a felted picture
of an elephant!

Sadly, my Mum had never got around to it.

I had not wanted anyone to touch Liana's hair, after
she died. Although I had thought how much I wanted
some of her beautiful hair, I just couldn't cut it. I
wanted her to remain as she was. Later I regretted
this decision, as her hair was such a defining feature;
just beautiful, and lots of it. So, this gift of Liana's hair
was simply overwhelming. The shiny brown waves
brought back so many memories, and I always feel
so lucky that my Mum did this for me!

The messages of validation continued through
the session – they were very comforting as well as

accurate. It gave me a lot of peace of mind to know that I could connect with Liana in this way. I was told that she knew that she was going to pass, and was at peace with it. This linked me to something that I had found after she died and which I had thought odd. I was packing up some of her personal bits, and inside her handbag was her diary for appointments. I browsed the pages and came to her birthday date for that year, 7th June 2015, when she would have been twenty-three – yet she had written twenty-two (22 with a balloon next to it). Why would she have got her own age wrong? It didn't make sense. She is of course, forever 22. Perhaps she knew?

When Liana was in her early teenage years, we used to watch psychic medium John Edward on the television together. It was again for validation of our personal beliefs, and he is a world-renowned psychic medium who has done lots of worldwide tours. I went to see him in 2009 with my now sister-in-law, and I was bowled over by his readings for people in the auditorium.

So, to see John Edward after Liana died was on my wish-list. He was in London doing shows, just a few weeks before I wrote this; and on 20th May 2018, at the Apollo Victoria, we went along to see him. I knew that Liana would be coming through him, even on the journey up there to London – I said to her, out loud in my car, 'Liana, this is the guy we used to watch together, so get your ass in gear and get up here and show me some validation!'

I could feel her in the auditorium, and I said to my sister-in-law, 'She's here''. John got on with his show, and very close to the end he came to me and connected with Liana.

I am happy to share what he said:

He asked me 'Who is Michael?'

I replied that he was my late uncle, who had passed away three months prior. I had been at the hospital when he died and had left the room just minutes before he passed.

John said, 'Michael acknowledges that you were there, and is grateful – he was very much a part of the church.'

He absolutely was!

John said, 'Whose is the name with the letters L & N as the consonants?'

I replied, 'That is Liana, my daughter who passed away three years ago.'

He talked about her acting out her role when she was here on this Earth, but he said that she is now able to really be herself. She had done what she needed to do, whilst here.

Then he held up his inner wrist in the air and said, 'What is this? Why is she telling me to hold up my wrist?'

I was able to tell him that when Liana was on life-support for the last time, just a couple of days before she left us, I had taken a photograph of the three initials that she'd had tattooed on her inner wrist before she had left for Uganda. I had gone across the road from the hospital to a tattoo parlour, to get the same letters tattooed on my wrist, too.

The initials were DLC (for Di, Liana & Caitlin). This allowed her to feel that she was taking us with her. Liana had always wanted us all three to have this tattoo, but both Caitlin and I had declined, as it wasn't the best of designs: but I felt that I needed to have it done now, and Caitlin had it done after Liana died.

John said, 'She is so happy about this!'

He then referenced the number of times she was on life-support: and that she knew that I had cared for her, moved her limbs and bathed her. She was grateful.

He then validated that she knew that they had wanted to give her a tracheostomy, to breathe, had she survived; but that I had made the right decision to let her go. She didn't want the tracheostomy, or the life that it would have meant.

John asked me if I had a third child, as Liana was saying that she is with a 'sister over there'. So, I was able to tell John that Liana's best friend Kayleigh, who had died fourteen months after Liana, was with her. Funnily enough, she is mentioned on Facebook as my 'daughter' since I called her my number three.

He then said that Liana wanted me to know that it was she who had knocked down the picture! – so if you read the whole story, you will already know what he is talking about!!

One of the final things he said was, 'Why is she asking about her sunglasses? What did you do with them?'

Oh dear! – the look on his face told me that I was in trouble! My reply made the audience in the auditorium laugh – 'I may have given her Rayban sunglasses to her sister?!' I said as I screwed up my face.

His reply of, 'Hmmm' told me that she wasn't best pleased (as she had been very 'precious' about them when she was alive).

What I couldn't tell him at that moment (as I only found out a couple of hours later, as I was travelling home) was that on that very morning, Caitlin had accidentally broken those sunglasses! She squirmed as she told me – and I imagine that she felt as though her sister had told a tale on her, even from heaven! Glasses repaired, Caitlin no longer wears them!

Other wonderfully personal validations came through that day: precise, exact, showing me that Liana was there: it was a wonderful time for me.

When you have lost a child, you could have validation daily – but it is never enough. It is always exciting, but it is still never enough – and it can never happen enough times. John's validation of what I already knew gave me a tremendous feeling of peace.

I hope that if you have lost a child, or anyone else you love, you can be open to this validation that they give. It is when you are open to it that it will come – and you will be so glad that you got it.

Of course, all of this above is just my personal feelings and beliefs. I appreciate many will not agree with them and I am totally happy with that. It would have been unfair not to share them with such a powerful story.

So, Who Is Our Hero?

I want to introduce our hero, Liana's donor, to you all in this story. You see, I now know who she is...

Liana had started to write a letter to the family of her donor in the late autumn on 2015, about eight months after transplant. She felt it was the right time. During that difficult writing process, she had sadly rejected the kidney, and was as you now know, very unwell.

She put the letter down and said she would finish it and send it (via the transplant co-ordinator system) once she was strong and able to tell them that everything was fine.

Of course, that day never came.

In the summer after Liana died, I decided to finish the letter for her. I wrote and told them what had now happened, that Liana had passed away but had been ever grateful for the chance of life again. I included the part letter that Liana had started as a gift to them so that they could see her handwriting, although it was shaky from so many immunosuppressants.

With this process of contact comes total obscurity. You are not allowed to identify yourself by using names and details, but I knew I had enough information in the letter that Liana was somehow identifiable. I wanted them to find me I guess. I talked about her trip to Africa at the age of 18 and how she had been an Olympic torch bearer in 2012.

You only must type 'Africa girl - Olympic torch - kidney transplant' into Google and Liana pops up every time.

A few weeks later I received a beautiful letter in return, telling me a little about our hero (but of course no personal details at that time) and how sorry the family were to hear our news and that they were so glad to hear how their daughter had been able to help.

But, our donor's sister had done exactly as I had hoped and Googled what she could, and Liana popped up!

Nothing then happened for at least another year. One night as I settled into bed I received a Facebook messenger notification; someone wanted to request to send me a message. Her name was Carol and she told me I didn't know her, but she believed we were linked through her sister's passing and she believed we had received a kidney from her.

She very gently explained that if her contact was in any way unwanted or painful that I was to accept her apology and she hoped to not have seemed rude. I instantly read her message over and over and hit the reply button. The link was made. We spent many days sending each other huge swathes of messages detailing our loved ones and how they lived and died. It was an amazing comfort and we are still in touch to this day.

We haven't met in person, although I feel that will happen one day when we are all ready. Our lives have all been very busy and we live a few hours away from each other. It is lovely to be linked to the family via Facebook and to see their beautiful family grow. To see that they too still laugh and love. That we can give them even a little comfort in their dark hours, knowing how much we love and honour them too.

I have asked our donors sister Carol to write a passage in her own words here.

Our beautiful donor, her name is Teresa.

From Carol:

My sister Teresa Elizabeth Houghton was named after my great Spanish aunt. She was born on the 31st October 1975. She had dark hair eyes and had a very Hispanic look about her.

As a child she was really into music. She used to lock herself in her room for hours on her Walkman listening to all sorts of music. I could hear the floor boards squeaking all the time and know she was dancing away - but she would never admit it!

Our first ever concert together was 'Bros' - it was amazing. I remember she had bottle tops on her Doc Martins which was the craze at the time! We then went on to see 'New Kids on the Block' together, twice!

As teenagers she kept herself to herself - we didn't fight - but she stayed out of my way as I suppose being three years younger I was the annoying little sister! We enjoyed many holidays to Spain visiting all our family, but I do remember our first package holiday to Greece when she was sixteen was one we both classed as our favourite. We were on our own just the four of us and my parents were completely relaxed. I have fond memories of my parents and Teresa sat on the apartment balcony having a pizza and wine, lots of laughing, it made me happy as she didn't often want to be with us.

We became very close again when she left home to go to university. She went to Sheffield Hallam and I remember the house feeling so strange and empty. I often would go into her bedroom just to feel a bit closer to her.

I visited her a few times there, where she showed me what university life was really like. I had my first cheesy chips on a night out! It was cool to be able to visit her and stay together with no parents in the house!

She then went on to do a master's in marketing at the University of Madrid. I flew out a couple of times to stay with her there and that is when it was very evident she knew how to party. She kept me out dancing one night until 7am!

She finished her masters and stayed in Madrid for a while working until she decided to come back to the UK to find a job and a house in London. Again, we had many nights out together partying - I loved going to stay with her.

I met my husband and we got married in 2005. One memory that stands out is at my wedding at the end she started to cry and continued to cry for 24 hours. I didn't understand why at the time, but I now know my mum said she had told her she felt like she had lost me.

My husband Richard and I continued to have nights out with Teresa, but she didn't always have a boyfriend, so the dynamics had changed.

I gave birth to my first child in 2007 and Teresa arrived at the hospital having got two trains from London just three hours later to meet her precious niece.

Teresa loved food, and she arrived at my hospital bed, after I had been in labour for 18 hours starving; with a sandwich for herself and a drink, and then polished off my hospital toast!

She was such a good aunt and spoiled Isabella rotten. She would glare at our mum if she held Isabella for too long not offering her back to her!

Teresa really got into cycling, it started with her cycling to work in London saying it was better for the environment and cheaper and she hated the tube trains. She then joined a cycling club much to our amazement, as she wasn't physically the fittest of people. Now I look back it was the best thing she could ever have done, she was single, all her friends around her were having families and it was a great hobby for her to get out at the weekends, keep fit and stay sociable.

She went on various cycling trips to the Pyrenees and would cycle many kilometres over multiple days, she was so fit! She ran two London marathons and cycled the route from London to Paris twice.

It all started to change in 2013. Our parents wanted to take us all on a cruise around the mediterranean, but she didn't want to come with us saying she just didn't feel she would fit in which was really hard to understand. She began to suffer from headaches and became increasingly 'difficult' to be around. She would sometime be a little aggressive with her words.

She had been to see a doctor several times and she would be prescribed different tablets. She was told that she was tense because of all the exercise she was doing. She had been booked into have an MRI scan in the August of 2013, but after a sports massage her headaches subsided so she cancelled it.

The headaches returned in the September, so she was booked in for another scan which she had a few weeks later in October.

I had a second child Luca who she again adored. In the early October of 2013 I arranged to visit her at her house. I called her at 9am to say we were on our way and we would arrive two hours later. I will never forget the look on her face when we arrived at 11am. She was still in her pyjamas and she was shocked that I had arrived. It seemed very odd. As we entered her flat in Camden it was in a disgusting state. It was then she explained that she was finding it difficult to keep on top of things. She kept forgetting everything.

Alarm bells starting ringing as she just wasn't right. For her birthday a couple of weeks later, she had booked herself into a spa for the day and asked if I could join her. I didn't have enough money so suggested she meet at mine after and we have dinner (she often had spas on her own- she was very comfortable in her own company, so it wasn't unusual).

One of my biggest regrets is not spending the day with her. She joined us that evening at mine and we all went out for a pizza, including my parents. Teresa told us she had a scan and they had found a slug like vein that was abnormal in her brain. She would need a biopsy to find out exactly what it was. We were all very worried, but she seemed very calm.

She had a biopsy in the November where they confirmed she had a brain tumour. It was in the part of her brain that affected quite a few vital nerves, so she was told to immediately stop driving, and was signed off work until further notice. She would need both chemotherapy and radiotherapy in December.

Once we got to December things didn't go in her favour. Just before treatment was about to start it was postponed as they decided they were now unsure of the grade of the tumour and that they needed a second biopsy. Christmas got in the way, the doctors didn't get back to her and nothing much was happening.

She spent Christmas that year in my house as I was 36 weeks pregnant with my third child. As we opened presents we saw she had duplicated a few, having absolutely no idea why. She had to go to bed to rest and slept for two hours. Her weight had ballooned because of the steroids – it was clear she wasn't well.

I was due to have a late pregnancy scan on the 20th of January and I asked Teresa to come with me. I'm so pleased I did, as she didn't have any children of her own and had never experienced a scan. Our mum, Teresa and I then went out for lunch. The restaurant was only a five-minute walk away, but Teresa was very breathless and got tired walking that short distance. We had a lovely meal, I drove them back to fetch their car. Little did I know that would be the last time I would see her conscious.

Teresa had her second brain biopsy booked in for the next day, the 21st of January 2014. Again, she was very calm and just keen to get treatment sorted.

I still have her messages she sent me - one of them declaring she was taking her own pillow with her, as the hospital ones were rubbish. The second message was her saying she had had a full wax and her nails painted just in case she died in the operating theatre! I told her she was being ridiculous!

Her biopsy went well, and she stayed in for two nights. She was about to be discharged from the ward when she suffered multiple seizures. The first lasting seven minutes.

Her health went down-hill that day and she had to be sedated as they could not keep the seizures under control. She was taken to intensive care on the 23rd of January as they wanted to keep a close eye on her.

On the Friday, 24th January, they attempted to remove the sedation to see how her body would respond. It became clear she could not breath on her own. On the Saturday morning our dad called me to say she would not survive. Her brain had reacted very badly to the biopsy, which caused the multiple seizures. She was now on life-support and we needed to discuss what to do next.

I jumped on the train and went straight to London (now 39 weeks pregnant). Nothing prepared me for what was to follow. Dad met me outside the hospital and before we went in he said, 'we are now in discussion of transplantation'.

In my pregnant hormonal state for about ten seconds I actually thought they were going to give her a new brain! Then I realised exactly what he had said. We entered the hospital and he asked me again, 'what do you think Teresa would feel about donating her organs?' I immediately replied, 'she was all pro-recycling so 100% let's do it', everyone laughed - which was weird in such awful circumstances.

The thing is, even though Teresa and I didn't always see eye to eye, especially in her final year when we didn't know she was ill, when she was behaving strangely and staying odd things (now we know it was the tumour) she was the most kind giving generous person. She was always putting her friends first. She would be the first to offer to cook for someone, she put so much thought into gifts - to make them personal - she would have 100% agreed to donate her organs and help someone else. She was on the organ donor list but it's not a conversation we had all had before.

She would have been so proud of how many people she helped, as are we.

I said my goodbyes to her early evening of the 25th and took the train home. I remember shaking on the train, sweating and feeling like my heart had just been torn out of me.

The next morning of the 26th January 2014, the medical team did one final brain activity test with my parents as witnesses, there was nothing. She was completely brain dead but the machine was still pumping so her heart and her organs were all still alive.

My mum called me as it was being announced her time of death.

I gave birth to my third child 5 days later, the 31st of January. I called her Clara Teresita (Spanish for little Teresa). I know she would have loved that.

...

I am so grateful to Carol and her family for providing a little insight into Teresa... Rest in only the deepest of peace beautiful Teresa, we will always carry you with us too x

My Final Thoughts

I hope that this book, her story, has been a gift
to you. Maybe it affected you somehow to reach
out to someone you love. Perhaps it offered you
the opportunity to see the joy in each day. If her
story made your eyes well up, I hope only because
you were able to feel her strength and not her
weaknesses. She had both, but she will want you to
remember her strength.

I hope you feel a little comfort, if you are
unfortunate enough to be in my 'club'. If you are,
then I know this pain. You are not alone and must
seek to find even a tiny glimpse of light in your
darkness. Reach out if you need help, either from a
GP or a friend or family member. Look hard enough
and you will see it, I promise you.

You can find more information at Cruse
Bereavement Care (somewhere to turn when
someone dies) on their website https://www.cruse.
org.uk or telephone 0808 808 1677.

I hope Liana's story has encouraged you to think a
little more about organ donation. It may be that you
are already registered on the UK donor list? Fantastic!

If not, it may be that you will be inspired to give
that gift of life when you no longer need it. You can
find more information and register if you wish on the
website: **https://www.organdonation.nhs.uk.**

The organ donation register is a confidential list
of people who want to donate their organs and/or

tissue. Even if your name is on the register, when you die, they will ask your family or friends to confirm that you had not changed your mind.

How to register
- Fill in an online form
- Call 0300 123 23 23

You can also join when you:
- Register for a driving licence
- Apply for a Boots Advantage card
- Register at a GP surgery
- Register for a European Health Insurance card (EHIC)

Note: As I write, this news has come forward that a new opt-out system for organ donation will be in place by 2020 in England, if Parliament approves 'Max's Law'. Under the plans detailed by ministers, adults will be presumed to be organ donors unless they have specifically recorded their decision not to be.

The government said it would save up to 700 lives each year. Whilst this is fantastic news, you still need to have the conversation with your loved ones as their wishes will still be able to override yours. Making sure they know what you want takes away some of their pain and uncertainty if that tough moment comes.

I worry that we do not speak openly enough of death that we all inevitably move towards. We might assume it only happens to others. Reality often feels uncomfortable, and to declare your willingness to donate your organs in order to give life to others means facing up to death. If you don't make your decision to donate clear, the doctors will ask the person closest to you what they think you wanted, so talk with your loved ones.

If I could convey in words the feeling of joy when the call for Liana's kidney came through, you would be amazed. If you are unsure of the impact you can have, then I invite you back to read the interview Liana gave to *The Sunday Times* in section 21 again. Her final words in that interview are here...

'It's like someone telling you you're going on the most amazing holiday of your life, but you don't know when. Pack a bag and get ready,' she says, blinking hard. 'It could be any time between now and never.'

Love you Li xx